11+ Maths

Numerical Reasoning

WORKBOOK 3

Dr Stephen C Curran

Edited by Dr Tandip Singh Mann & Anne-Marie Choong

This book belongs to

Accelerated Education Publications Ltd.

Contents

9. Percentages   Pages

1.	What is a Percentage?	3-5
2.	Percentages and Fractions	6-16
3.	Percentage Calculations	16-17
4.	Percentage to Amount	17-24
5.	Amount to Percentage	25-28
6.	Mixed % Calculations	28-29
7.	Profit and Loss	29-32
8.	VAT (Value Added Tax)	32-34
9.	Two Percentages	34-35
10.	Mixed Percentage Problems	35-38
11.	Percentages and Decimals	39-41
12.	Fractions, Decimals and Percentages	42-46

10. Ratio and Proportion

1.	What is a Ratio?	47
2.	Comparing with the Whole	47-49
3.	Comparing with another Quantity	49-51
4.	Ratio and Proportion	52-53
5.	Amount to Ratio	54-59
6.	Ratio to Amount	59-65
7.	Other Ratio Types	65-71
8.	Maps and Scale Drawings	71-77
9.	Gradients	77-80
10.	Mixed Ratio Problems	81-82

© 2006 Stephen Curran

Chapter Nine
PERCENTAGES
1. What is a Percentage?

A **Percentage** is part of **100**.
One hundred per cent is the whole.

A percentage is indicated by this sign: **%**

Large and complex numbers can be reduced to parts of a hundred to make them easier to understand.

We see percentages displayed in shops, banks and on advertisements, and they are used for tax purposes.

Examples:

£120 + VAT at 20%

SALE
Fancy Dress Shop
15% off all items

Percentages can be shown on a grid of **100** squares.

1%
1 part of a hundred.

10%
10 parts of a hundred.

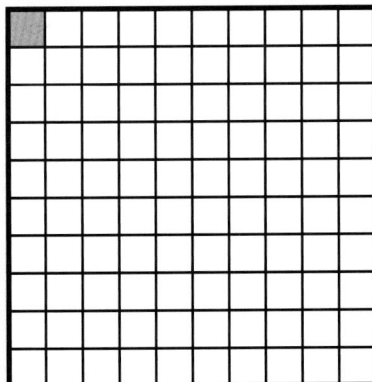
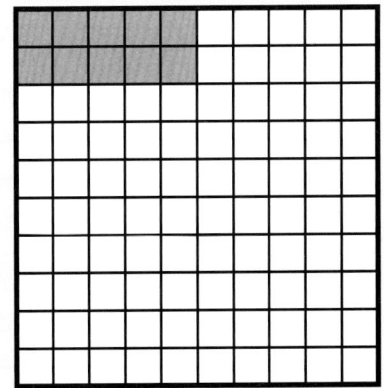

© 2006 Stephen Curran

Exercise 9: 1

Count the squares and write the % shaded in the space:

1) ____%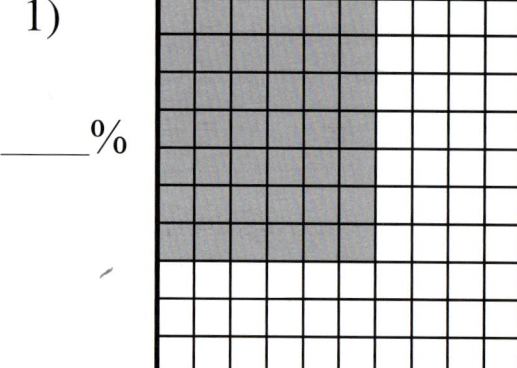

2) ____%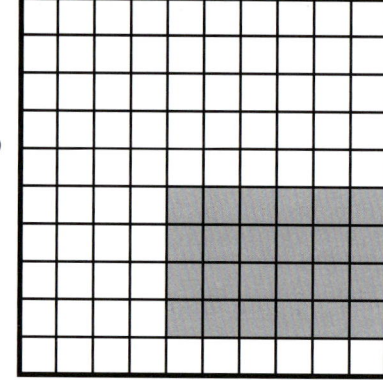

3) ____%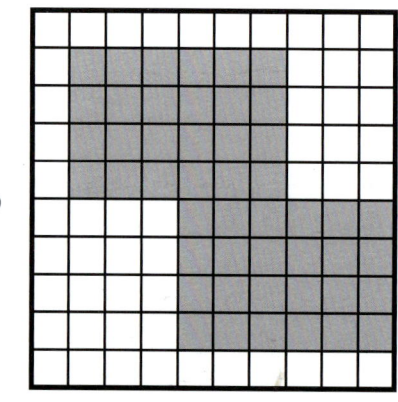

4) ____%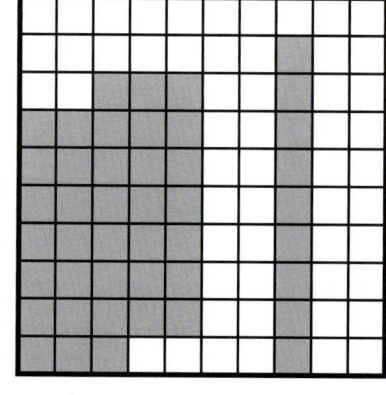

Shade in the percentages shown below:

5) **32%**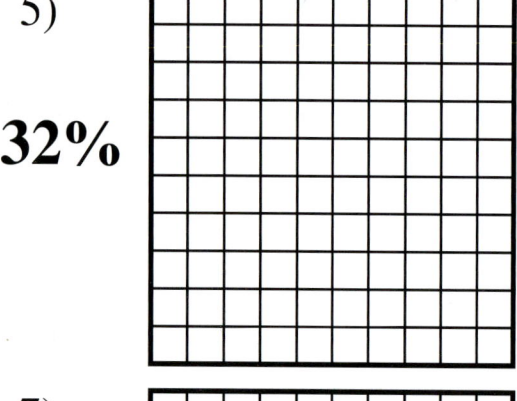

6) **23%**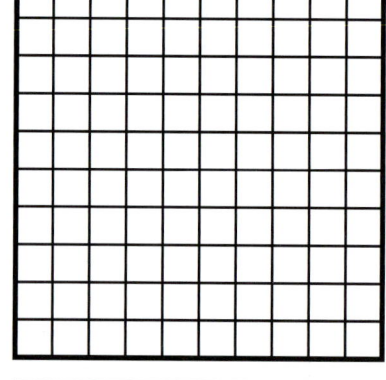

7) **12%**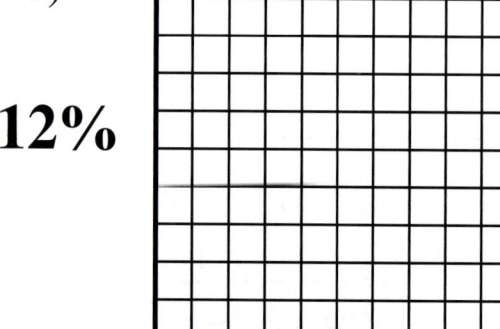

8) **55%**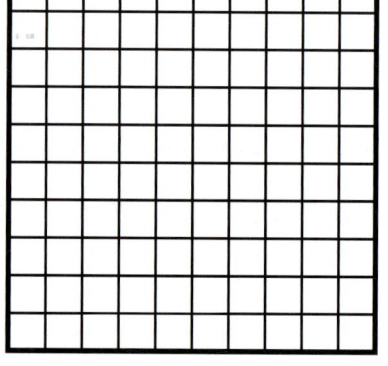

© 2006 Stephen Curran

9) A boy called Simon Cooper was asked to shade his initials on a grid of **100** squares.

What percentage do they take up on the grid? _____%

10) Shade in the initials of your name on the grid below:

What percentage of the grid do your initials take up?

_____ %

Record scores out of ten here →

2. Percentages and Fractions

A percentage can be expressed as a **Fraction**:

Examples:

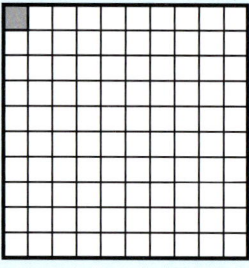
$1\% = \dfrac{1}{100}$

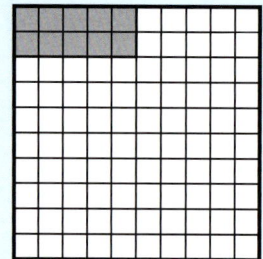
$10\% = \dfrac{1}{10}$

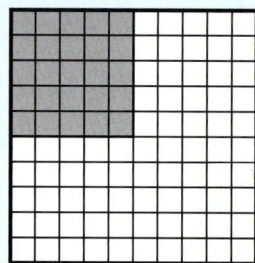
$25\% = \dfrac{1}{4}$

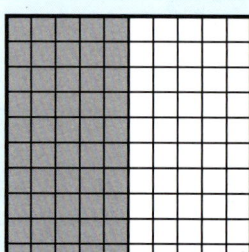
$50\% = \dfrac{1}{2}$

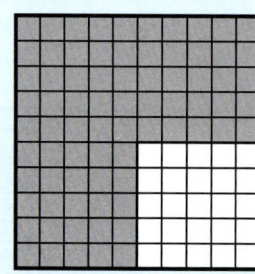
$75\% = \dfrac{3}{4}$

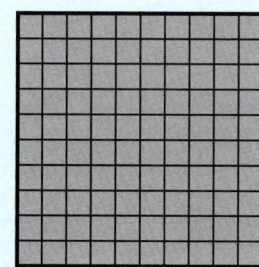
$100\% = 1$ whole

a. Changing Percentages to Fractions

(i) Ordinary Percentage to Fraction

Example: Convert **70%** to a fraction.

Divide by **10** (simplify).

$70 \div 100$

Divide by **10**

$\dfrac{\cancel{70}^{\,7}}{\cancel{100}^{\,10}} = \dfrac{7}{10}$

Therefore $70\% = \dfrac{7}{10}$

70 hundredths
(70 parts of 100)

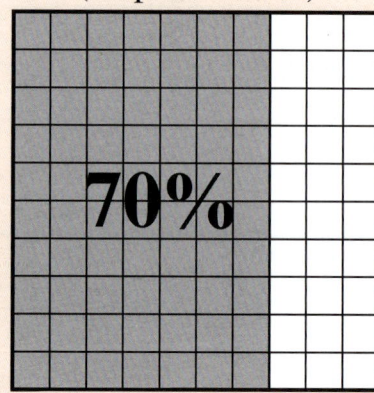

70%

© 2006 Stephen Curran

Exercise 9: 2 Change from % to fraction:

1) 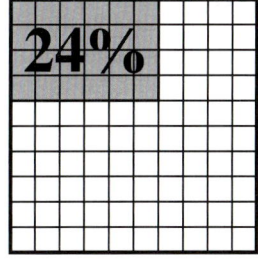 Simplify $\dfrac{24}{100}$ = ____

2) 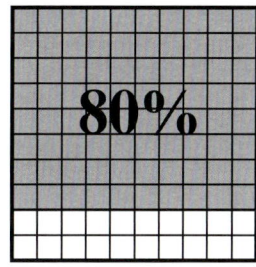 Simplify $\dfrac{80}{100}$ = ____

3) 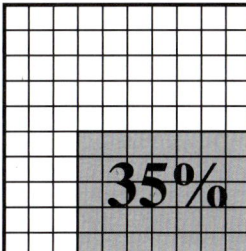 Simplify = ____

4) 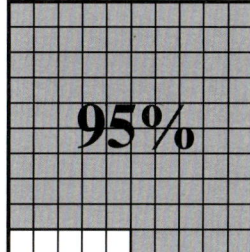 Simplify = ____

5) 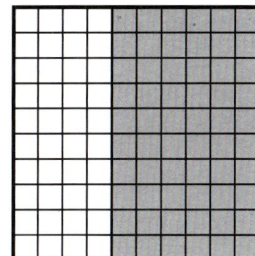 = ____

6) 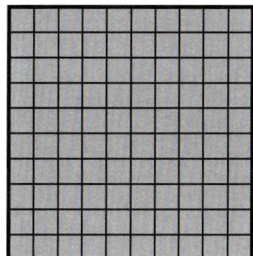 = ____

7) 16% = _____   8) 40% = _____

9) 39% = _____   10) 72% = _____

(ii) Whole Number Percentage to Mixed Number

Percentages bigger than a whole one have more than one hundred parts. They can be represented diagrammatically. For example:

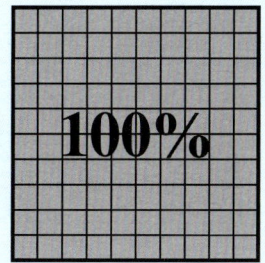 = 125%

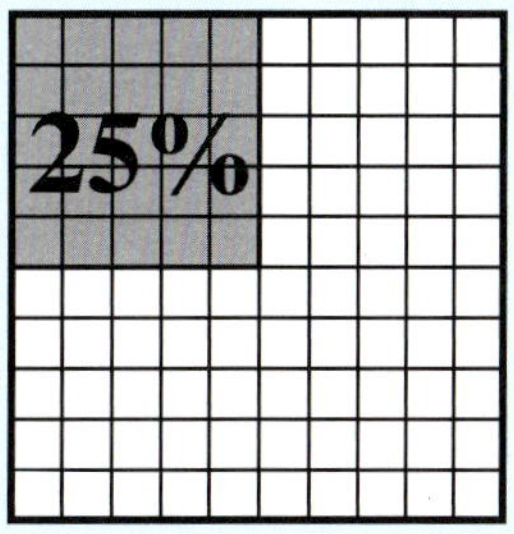

© 2006 Stephen Curran

Whole Number % to Mixed Number

Example: Convert **275%** to a mixed number.

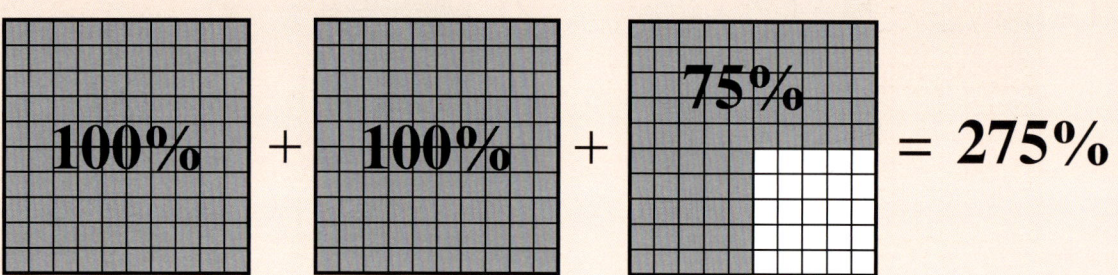 = 275%

1. Write as a fraction of **100**. $\dfrac{275}{100}$

2. Simplify (divide). $\dfrac{275}{100} \overset{\text{Divide by 25}}{=} \dfrac{11}{4}$

3. This is an improper fraction. $\dfrac{11}{4} \uparrow \text{Divide} = 2\dfrac{3}{4}$

Therefore $275\% = 2\dfrac{3}{4}$

Exercise 9: 3   Change from whole number % to mixed numbers:

1)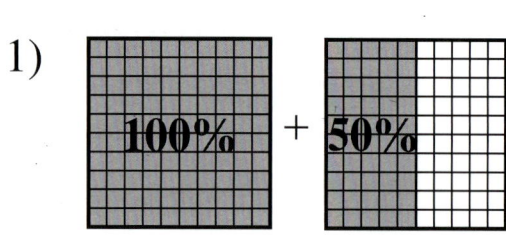

$= 150\% = \dfrac{150}{100}\,{}^3_2$

$= \dfrac{3}{2} \uparrow \text{Divide}$

$= \underline{}$

2)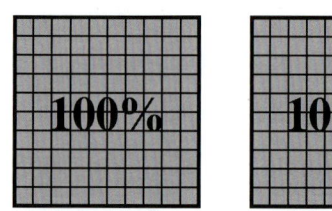

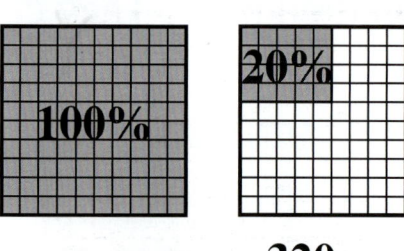

$= 320\% = \dfrac{320}{100}$

$= \underline{}$

© 2006 Stephen Curran

3)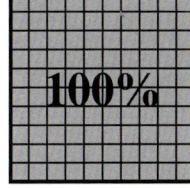

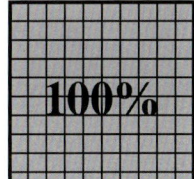 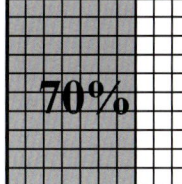

= 370% = _____

4)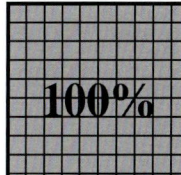

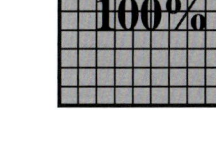 

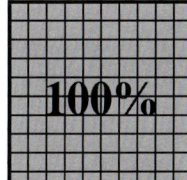

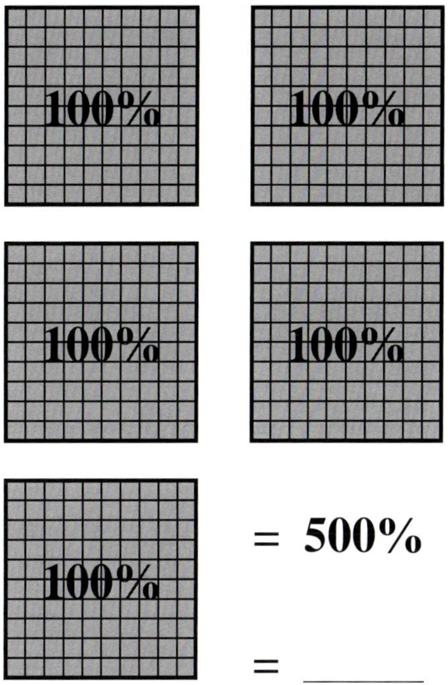

= 500%

= _____

5)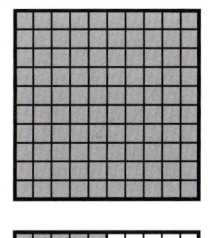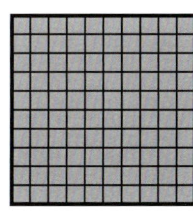

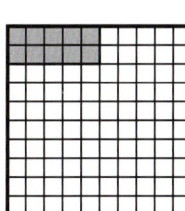

= _____

6)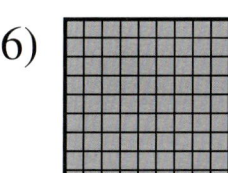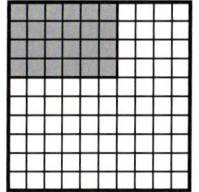

= _____

7) 315% = _____   8) 675% = _____

9) 105% = _____   10) 460% = _____

Score

(iii) Mixed Number Percentage to Fraction

Percentages containing a whole number and a fraction can be termed **Mixed Number** or **Fractional Percentages**.

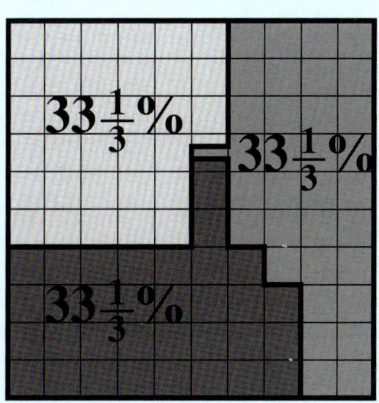

The grid has been divided into **3** main sections. Each section has **33** and $\frac{1}{3}$ parts shaded.

Each shaded part of this grid is

$33\frac{1}{3}$% or $\frac{1}{3}$ of the whole.

© 2006 Stephen Curran

Mixed number or fractional percentages occur because many numbers will not divide exactly into **100**.

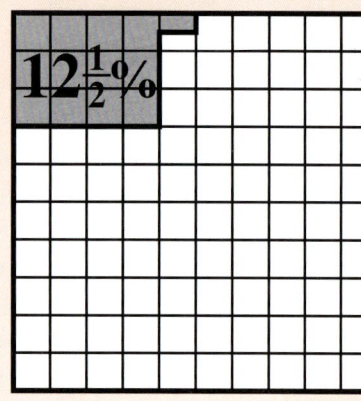

Example: $\boxed{12\frac{1}{2}\% \text{ as a fraction.}}$

This percentage cannot be made into a fraction in its present form.

$$\frac{12\frac{1}{2}\%}{100}$$ It will not simplify, as it is a fraction of a fraction.

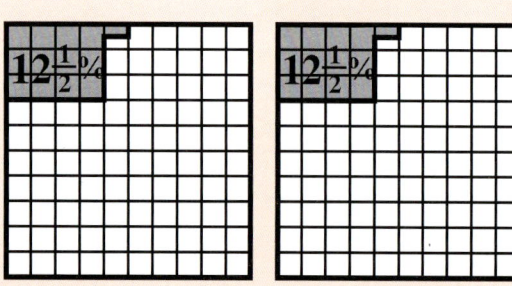

If the whole fraction is multiplied by **2**, the half is eliminated.

$$\frac{12\frac{1}{2}\% \times 2}{100 \times 2}$$

There are **25** squares shaded.
There are **200** squares in total.

Simplify $\dfrac{\cancel{25}^{\,1}}{\cancel{200}_{\,8}} = \dfrac{1}{8}$

Therefore $12\frac{1}{2}\% = \dfrac{1}{8}$

Mixed Number % to Fraction

(This method achieves the same as the above and is easier to remember.)

1. Convert to an improper fraction. $12\frac{1}{2}\% = \dfrac{25}{2}$

2. Multiply the denominator by **100**. $\dfrac{25}{2 \times 100} = \dfrac{25}{200}$

3. Simplify the fraction.   Divide by 25 $\dfrac{\cancel{25}^{\,1}}{\cancel{200}_{\,8}} = \dfrac{1}{8}$

Exercise 9: 4 Change the mixed number % to a fraction:  Score

1) $3\frac{1}{3}\% = $ _____   2) $37\frac{1}{2}\% = $ _____

3) $66\frac{2}{3}\% = $ _____   4) $16\frac{2}{3}\% = $ _____

5) $87\frac{1}{2}\% = $ _____   6) $6\frac{1}{4}\% = $ _____

7) $62\frac{1}{2}\% = $ _____   8) $8\frac{1}{3}\% = $ _____

9) $83\frac{1}{3}\% = $ _____   10) $6\frac{2}{3}\% = $ _____

b. Changing Fractions to Percentages

(i) Fraction to Ordinary Percentage

Example: Change $\frac{7}{10}$ into a percentage.

Multiply by **100** (cancel).

$$\frac{7}{10} \times 100$$

Divide by 10

$$\frac{7}{\cancel{10}^{1}} \times \frac{\cancel{100}^{10}}{1} = \frac{70}{1}$$

Divide by 10

Therefore $\frac{7}{10} = 70\%$

7 tenths
(7 parts of 10)

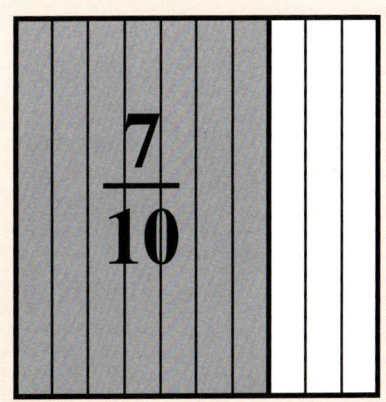

© 2006 Stephen Curran

Exercise 9: 5 Change from fraction to %:

Score

1)  $\dfrac{4}{5}$ Cancel $\dfrac{4}{5} \times \dfrac{100}{1}$

= _____ %

2) $\dfrac{9}{10}$ Cancel $\dfrac{9}{10} \times \dfrac{100}{1}$

= _____ %

3)  $\dfrac{9}{25}$ Cancel

= _____ %

4)  $\dfrac{13}{20}$ Cancel

= _____ %

5) 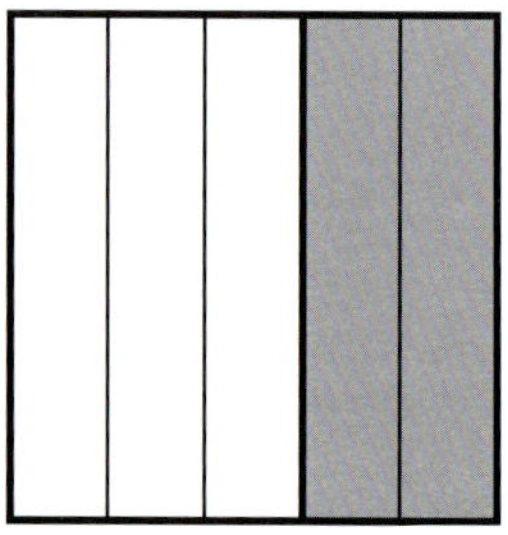 = _____ %

6) 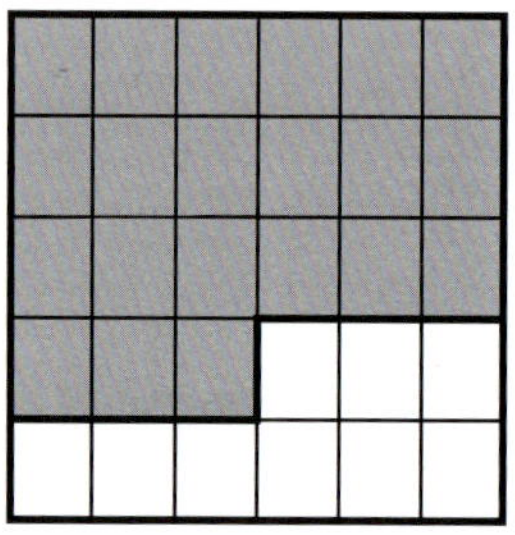 = _____ %

7) $\dfrac{19}{20}$ = _____ %   8) $\dfrac{9}{50}$ = _____ %

9) $\dfrac{9}{30}$ = _____ %   10) $\dfrac{17}{25}$ = _____ %

(ii) Mixed Number to Percentage

A whole one and a fraction is a mixed number and can be converted to a percentage.

Example:

Show $1\tfrac{1}{4}$ as a diagram.

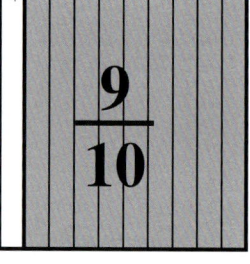

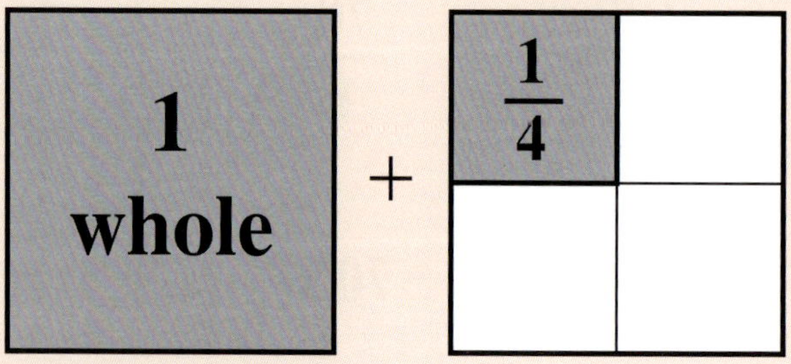

1 whole + $\tfrac{1}{4}$ = $1\tfrac{1}{4}$

12   © 2006 Stephen Curran

Mixed Number to %

Example: $2\frac{3}{4}$ as a percentage.

$$1 \text{ whole} + 1 \text{ whole} + \frac{3}{4} = 2\frac{3}{4}$$

1. Convert to an improper fraction. $2\frac{3}{4} = \frac{11}{4}$

2. Multiply by **100** (cancel). $\frac{11}{\cancel{4}_1} \times \frac{\cancel{100}^{25}}{1}$ Divide by 4

Therefore $2\frac{3}{4} = 275\%$

Exercise 9: 6   Change from mixed number to %:

1)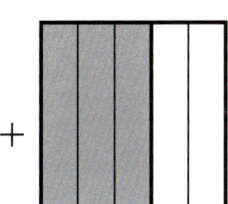

$= 1\frac{3}{5}$

$= \frac{8}{5} \times \frac{100}{1}$

$= \underline{}\%$

2)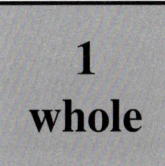

$= 3\frac{7}{10}$

$= \underline{}\%$

© 2006 Stephen Curran

3)   [1 whole] [1 whole]   4) [1 whole] [1 whole]

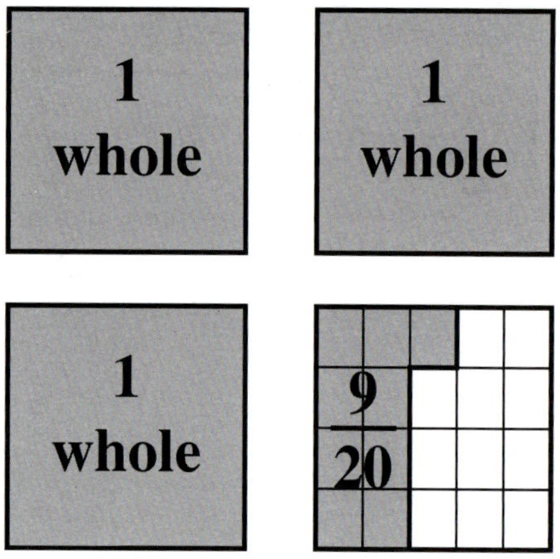

   [1 whole] [1 whole]   [1 whole]

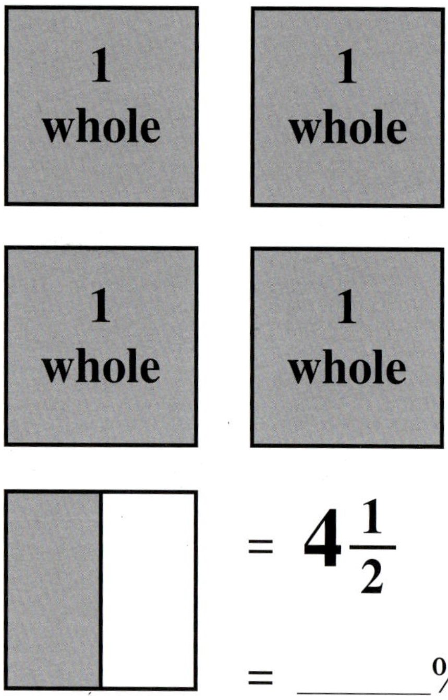

   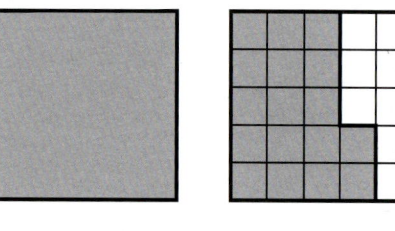 = $4\frac{1}{2}$ = _____ %

   = _____ %

                              6) [grey square] [grey square]

5) [grey square] [grid]

                                 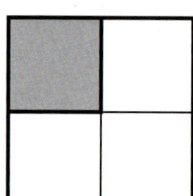

   = _____ %   = _____ %

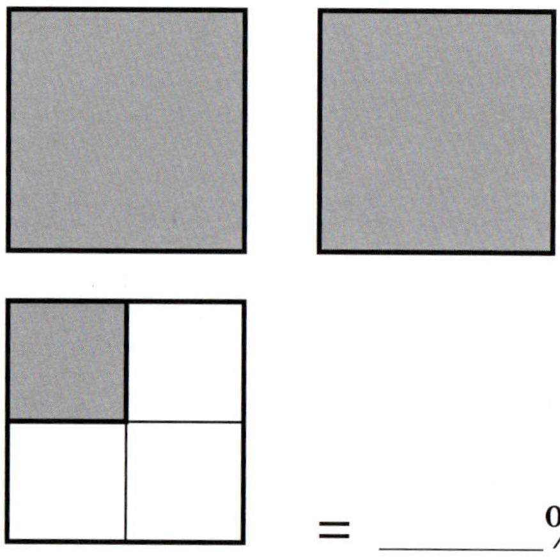

7) $1\frac{1}{20}$ = _____ %   8) $1\frac{3}{25}$ = _____ %   Score

9) $3\frac{3}{10}$ = _____ %   10) $2\frac{1}{5}$ = _____ %

(iii) Fraction to Mixed Number Percentage

Mixed Number Percentages will convert to a fraction.

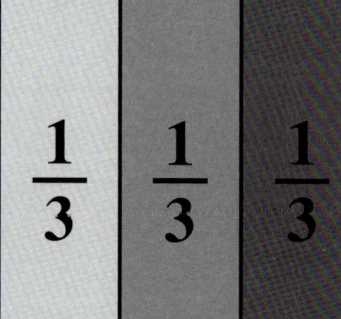 The grid has been divided into **3** main sections. Each section has one third shaded.

Each shaded part of this grid is

$\frac{1}{3}$ or $33\frac{1}{3}$% of the whole.

14   © 2006 Stephen Curran

100 cannot be exactly divided into 8 parts without a remainder. As a percentage it will result in whole ones and a fraction (a mixed number or fractional percentage).

$$\frac{1}{8} = 12\frac{1}{2}\% \quad \text{Mixed number \%}$$

Fraction to Mixed Number %

Example: $\frac{1}{8}$ as a percentage.

1. Multiply by **100** (cancel).

$$\frac{1}{\cancel{8}_2} \times \frac{\cancel{100}^{25}}{1} = \frac{25}{2} \quad \text{Divide by 4}$$

2. This is an improper fraction.

$$\frac{25}{2} \uparrow \text{Divide} = 12\frac{1}{2}$$

Therefore $\frac{1}{8} = 12\frac{1}{2}\%$

Exercise 9: 7   Change from fractions to mixed number %:

1)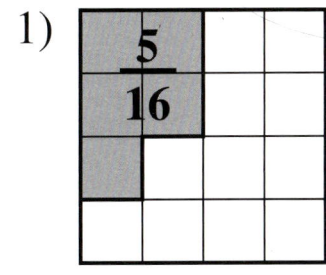

Cancel

$$\frac{5}{16} \times \frac{100}{1}$$

$$\frac{125}{4} \uparrow \text{Divide}$$

= _____ %

2)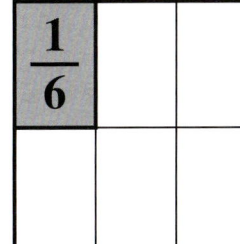

Cancel

$$\frac{1}{6} \times \frac{100}{1}$$

$$\frac{50}{3} \uparrow \text{Divide}$$

= _____ %

© 2006 Stephen Curran

3) 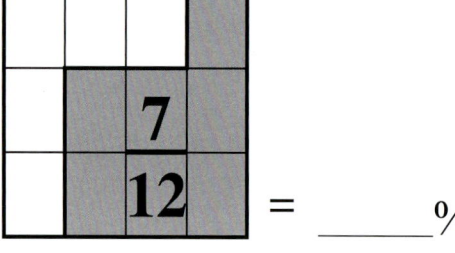 $\dfrac{7}{12}$ = ____ %

4)  $\dfrac{7}{8}$ = ____ %

5) $\dfrac{11}{15}$ = ____ %

6) $\dfrac{5}{6}$  = ____ %

7) $\dfrac{1}{15}$ = ____ %

8) $\dfrac{5}{12}$ = ____ %

9) $\dfrac{3}{8}$ = ____ %

10) $\dfrac{14}{15}$ = ____ %

3. Percentage Calculations

The conversion of percentages to fractions and fractions to percentages is the basis of all **Percentage Calculations**.

% to Fraction

Example: Convert **80%** to a fraction.

Divide by **100** (then simplify). $\dfrac{80}{100} = \dfrac{4}{5}$

Fraction to %

Example: Change $\dfrac{4}{5}$ into a percentage.

Multiply by **100** (then cancel). $\dfrac{4}{5} \times \dfrac{100}{1} = 80\%$

Percentage to Fraction becomes **Percentage to Amount**.
Fraction to Percentage becomes **Amount to Percentage**.
All percentage calculations are of two types:

either

Percentage to Amount   % ⟶ Amount

A percentage is given and an amount has to be found.
There are four types of question:

1. Basic % to amount - e.g. Find **20%** of **£440**.
2. Increasing amount by % - e.g. Increase **£55** by **32%**.
3. Decreasing amount by % - e.g. Decrease **£60** by **40%**.
4. Reverse % (Find an original amount or **100%**) - e.g.
   If **65%** of a number is **260**, what is the whole amount?

or

Amount to Percentage   Amount ⟶ %

An amount is given and a percentage has to be found.
There are three types of question:

1. Basic amount to % - e.g. What % is **30** out of **200**?
2. % increase - e.g. **£40** is increased to **£50**.
   Find the % it increased by.
3. % decrease - e.g. **£80** is decreased to **£8**.
   Find the % it decreased by.

4. Percentage to Amount
a. Basic Percentage to Amount

Simple % Calculations
These can be used to help find easy percentages.

 10% - find one tenth   - **divide by 10**
 20% - find one fifth   - **divide by 5**
 25% - find a quarter   - **divide by 4**
 50% - find a half   - **divide by 2**

© 2006 Stephen Curran

Example: Find 25% of 120.

To find **25%** is the same as finding one quarter.

Divide by **4**   120 ÷ 4 = 30

25% of 120 = 30

Other percentages can be found in two or three stages.

Example: Find **35%** of **£250**.

1. Find **10%** - divide by **10**   £250 ÷ 10 = £25
2. Find **30%** - multiply by **3**   £25 × 3 = £75
3. Find **35%** - add **5%**   £75 + £12.50 = £87.50

35% of £250 = £87.50

Exercise 9: 8   Find the following amounts:

Score

1) **40%** of **20**. _____
2) **20%** of **30**. _____
3) **85%** of **200**. _____
4) **90%** of **500**. _____
5) **25%** of **672**. _____
6) **30%** of **24g**. _____ g
7) **65%** of **£2.60**. £ _____
8) **70%** of **£16**. £ _____
9) **75%** of **18m**. _____ m
10) **60%** of **£9.50**. £ _____

Find an Amount from a %

This is a standard technique for finding percentages.

Example: Find **36%** of **250**.

Remember **of** is always ×

1. Write the % and amount as a fraction.

$$36\% = \frac{36}{100} \; \substack{\%}$$

$$250 = \frac{250}{1} \; \substack{\text{Amount}}$$

% ⟶ Amount

2. Multiply (cancel) the amount by the percentage.

$$\frac{36}{100}_2 \times \frac{\overset{5}{\cancel{250}}}{1} \quad \text{Divide by 50}$$

3. Simplify the fractions.

$$\frac{\overset{18}{\cancel{36}}}{\cancel{2}_1} \times \frac{5}{1} \quad \text{Divide by 2}$$

4. Multiply out the fractions.

$$\frac{18}{1} \times \frac{5}{1}$$

36% of 250 = 90

Exercise 9: 9a   Find the amount:

1) **30% of 960p.**

   £ _____

2) **80% of £625.**

   £ _____

3) **12% of 175cm.**

   _____ cm

4) **26% of 150km.**

   _____ km

© 2006 Stephen Curran

Find an Amount from a Whole Number %

Example: Find **125%** of **£52**.

$$\% \longrightarrow \text{Amount}$$

Cancel, simplify and multiply out.

$$\frac{\cancel{125}^{\ 5}}{\cancel{100}_{\ 1}} \times \frac{\cancel{52}^{\ 13}}{1}$$

$$125\% = £65$$

Exercise 9: 9b   Find the amount:

5) **204%** of **325g**.   6) **105%** of **£250**.

_____ g   £ _____

Find an Amount from a Mixed Number %

Example: Find $37\frac{1}{2}\%$ of **£80**.

$$\% \longrightarrow \text{Amount}$$

1. Convert mixed number % into an improper fraction.

$$\frac{75}{2}\% \times \frac{80}{1}$$

2. Multiply the denominator by **100**.

$$\frac{75}{2 \times 100} \times \frac{80}{1}$$

3. Cancel, simplify and multiply out.

$$\frac{\cancel{75}^{\ 3}}{\cancel{200}_{\ 1}} \times \frac{\cancel{80}^{\ 10}}{1}$$

$$37\tfrac{1}{2}\% \text{ of } £80 = £30$$

Exercise 9: 9c   Find the amount: Score

7) $12\frac{1}{2}\%$ of **64p**.

_____ p

8) $6\frac{1}{4}\%$ of **£80**.

£ _____

9) $62\frac{1}{2}\%$ of **144cm**.

_____ cm

10) $16\frac{2}{3}\%$ of **90km**.

_____ km

b. Increasing Amounts by Percentage

Amounts can be **Increased by a Percentage**.

Example: Increase **£40** by **10%**.

Method 1   % → Amount

1. Find **10%** of **£40**.

$$\frac{\cancel{10}^{\,1}}{\cancel{100}_{\,\cancel{10}_{\,1}}} \times \frac{\cancel{40}^{\,4}}{1}$$

10% of **£40** = **£4**

2. Add the amount onto the original amount.

£40 + **£4** = **£44**

£40 increased by **10%** = **£44**

Method 2

1. Add the **10%** on at the beginning.

100% + 10% = 110%

% → Amount

2. Find **110%** of **£40**.

$$\frac{\cancel{110}^{\,11}}{\cancel{100}_{\,\cancel{10}_{\,1}}} \times \frac{\cancel{40}^{\,4}}{1}$$

£40 increased by **10%** = **£44**

Exercise 9: 10a What is the new amount?

1) Increase **90p** by **20%**.   2) Increase **£25** by **30%**.

£ _____   £ _____

Increase the following amounts by **25%**:

3) **180cm**   4) **17.6km**   5) **420m**

= _____ cm   = _____ km   = _____ m

c. Decreasing Amounts by Percentage

Amounts can be **Decreased by a Percentage**.

Example: Decrease **150** by **5%**.

Method 1   % ⟶ Amount

1. Find **5%** of **150**. $\dfrac{5}{\cancel{100}^{\,2}} \times \dfrac{\cancel{150}^{\,3}}{1}$

This is an improper fraction. $\dfrac{15}{2}$ ↑ Divide

$15 \div 2 = 7.5$

5% of **150** = **7.5**

2. Subtract from the original amount. $150 - 7.5 = 142.5$

150 decreased by **5%** = **142.5**

Method 2

1. Subtract the **5%** at the beginning.

$$100\% - 5\% = 95\%$$

2. Find **95%** of **150**.

% → Amount

$$\frac{\cancel{95}^{19}}{\cancel{100}^{20}_{2}} \times \frac{\cancel{150}^{15}}{1}$$

This is an improper fraction.

$$\frac{285}{2} \uparrow \text{Divide}$$

150 decreased by **5%** = **142.5**

Exercise 9: 10b What is the new amount?

6) Decrease **60p** by **20%**.
_____ p

7) Decrease **£40** by **30%**.
£ _____

Decrease the following amounts by **35%**:

8) **120cm**   9) **20km**   10) **140m**

= _____ cm   = _____ km   = _____ m

d. Reverse Percentage

To find the original amount (100%) from a given percentage.

Example: 425 is **85%** of which number?

1% of the number can be written as: $\dfrac{425}{85}$

Find the number. Multiply by **100%** $\dfrac{100}{1}$

It can be be expressed as: % ⟶ Amount

1. Cancel and simplify the fractions.

$$\frac{\cancel{100}^{20}}{1} \times \frac{\cancel{425}^{25}}{\cancel{85}_{\cancel{17}\,1}}$$

2. Multiply out the fractions. $25 \times 20 = 500$

The original amount is **500**.

Exercise 9: 11   Find the original amount (100%):

1) **150** is **60%** of which number?

   % ⟶ Am

   $$\frac{100}{1} \times \frac{150}{60} \,\underline{\quad\quad}$$

2) What is the whole amount if **574** is **70%**?

   % ⟶ Am

   $$\frac{100}{1} \times \frac{574}{70} \,\underline{\quad\quad}$$

3) What is **100%** if **45%** is **£108**? £ _____

4) If **55%** is **165km**, what is **100%**? _____ km

5) What is the whole amount if **190p** is **40%**? £ _____

6) What is the whole amount if **52cm** is **20%**? _____ cm

7) What is **100%** if **65%** is **104m**? _____ m

8) If **30%** is **£21**, what is **100%**? £ _____

9) **56g** is **16%** of which number? _____ g

10) What is **100%** if **5%** is **3p**? _____ p

5. Amount to Percentage
a. Basic Amount to Percentage

Find a % from an Amount

This involves converting an amount to a percentage.

Example: What percentage of **220** is **44**?

1. Write the amount and % as a fraction and multiply. (Cancel)

   Amount   %
   $\frac{44}{220}$ $\frac{100}{1}$

   Amount $\longrightarrow$ %

   Divide by **20**

   $= \frac{44}{220}^{11} \times \frac{\cancel{100}^{5}}{1}$

   Divide by **11**

2. Simplify the fractions.

   $= \frac{\cancel{44}^{4}}{\cancel{11}^{1}} \times \frac{5}{1}$

3. Multiply out the fractions.

   $= \frac{4}{1} \times \frac{5}{1}$

44 as a % of 220 = 20%

Exercise 9: 12a Find the %:

1) **150g** as a % of **1000g**.

   _____%

2) **85p** as a % of **£5**.

   _____%

3) **£90** as a % of **£250**.

   _____%

4) **42m** as a % of **210m**.

   _____%

© 2006 Stephen Curran

Find a Whole Number % from an Amount

Example: £70 compared in % terms to £40.

Amount ⟶ %

Cancel, simplify and multiply out.

$$\frac{\cancel{70}^{35}}{\cancel{40}_{\cancel{2}_1}} \times \frac{\cancel{100}^{5}}{1}$$

£70 = 175%

Exercise 9: 12b Find the whole number %:

5) **112g** compared as a % to **32g**.

_____%

6) **£62.50** compared as a % to **£25**.

_____%

Find a Mixed Number % from an Amount

Example: £50 as a % of £80.

Amount ⟶ %

Cancel, simplify and multiply out.

$$\frac{\cancel{50}^{25}}{\cancel{80}_{\cancel{4}_2}} \times \frac{\cancel{100}^{5}}{1}$$

This is an improper fraction.

$$\frac{125}{2} \xrightarrow{\text{Divide}} = 62\tfrac{1}{2}\%$$

£50 as a % of £80 = $62\tfrac{1}{2}$%

Exercise 9: 12c Find the mixed number %:

Score

7) **14m** as a % of **32m**.

_____%

8) **60g** as a % of **144g**.

_____%

9) **3km** as a % of **8km**.

_____%

10) **£25** as a % of **£30**.

_____%

b. Percentage Increase and Decrease

Finding out the percentage an amount has increased by:

Example: **£720** is increased to **£828**. By what percentage has it increased?

1. Find out the difference in amount by subtraction.

$$828 - 720 = 108$$

2. Express the new amount as a fraction of the original amount.

$$\frac{108}{720}$$

3. Amount to % calculation.
Amount ⟶ %

$$= \frac{\cancel{108}^{3}}{\cancel{720}_{\cancel{36}_{1}}} \times \frac{\cancel{100}^{5}}{1}$$

The percentage increase is **15%**.

A percentage decrease is done in exactly the same way.

Example: **£500** is decreased to **£375**. By what percentage has it decreased?

1. Subtract.
500 − 375 = 125

2. Calculation. $\frac{^{25}\cancel{125}}{_{1\cancel{5}}\cancel{500}} \times \frac{\cancel{100}^{1}}{1}$

The percentage decrease is **25%**.

Exercise 9: 13 Calculate the percentage increase or decrease if:

40kg is increased to: 1) **65kg** ___ % 2) **72kg** ___ %

£800 is decreased to: 3) **£640** ___ % 4) **£30** ___ %

60kg is increased to: 5) **78kg** ___ % 6) **72kg** ___ %

£120 is decreased to: 7) **£96** ___ % 8) **£90** ___ %

£800 is decreased to: 9) **£500** ___ % 10) **£120** ___ %

6. Mixed % Calculations

Exercise 9: 14 Calculate the following:

Percentage to amount questions.

1) **65%** of **£2.80**.

2) **12%** of **350cm**.

£ _____

_____ cm

3) What is $16\frac{2}{3}$**%** of **270km**?

4) Increase **£1.80** by **45%**.

_____ km

£ _____

5) Decrease **£2.20** by **30%**.

6) What is the whole amount if **380km** is **40%**?

£ _____

_____ km

Amount to percentage questions.

7) **£180** as a % of **£500**.   8) **3km** as a % of **24km**.

_____%   _____%

9) Give the % decrease if **80km** is reduced to **50km**.   10) Give the % increase if **£32** is increased to **£40**.

_____%   _____%

7. Profit and Loss
a. Finding an Original Cost Price

Finding an Original Cost Price from a percentage profit or loss uses the same calculation as a reverse percentage.

An Original Cost from a Percentage Profit

Example: A shopkeeper sells a television for **£150**, making a **20%** profit. What is the original cost price of the television?

The original cost price is always **100%** or $\frac{100}{1}$.

The selling price is **£150**. (**100% + 20% = 120%**)   Divide amount by %. $= \frac{150}{120}$

It can be expressed as: % → Amount

1. Cancel and simplify the fractions.

$$\frac{\cancel{100}^{\,5}}{1} \times \frac{\cancel{150}^{\,25}}{\cancel{120}_{\,1}^{\,\cancel{6}}}$$

2. Multiply out the fractions. $5 \times 25 = £125$

© 2006 Stephen Curran

An Original Cost from a Percentage Loss

Example: The same shopkeeper sells a table for **£63**, making a **30%** loss. What is the original cost price of the table?

The original cost price is always **100%** or $\frac{100}{1}$.

The selling price is **£63**. Divide amount by %. $= \frac{63}{70}$
(**100% − 30% = 70%**)

It can be be expressed as: % ⟶ Amount

1. Cancel and simplify the fractions.

$$\frac{\cancel{100}^{10}}{1} \times \frac{\cancel{63}^{9}}{\cancel{70}_{1}}$$

2. Multiply out the fractions. **10 × 9 = £90**

Exercise 9: 15a   Calculate the following:

1) A store sells a radio for **£156**. If the profit is **30%**, the cost price is £ _____ .

$$\frac{\%}{1} \longrightarrow \frac{Am}{1} \qquad \frac{100}{1} \times \frac{156}{130}$$

2) An art dealer sells a painting for **£3,500**, making a **40%** profit. How much did he originally pay for it? £ _____

3) A girl buys **10** bottles of perfume, then sells them for **£2.40** each, making **60%** profit. What did she originally pay for the pack of **10** bottles? £ _____

4) A man sold his car for **£2,700**, making a **20%** loss. The original cost was £ _____ .

$$\frac{\%}{1} \longrightarrow Am \qquad \frac{100}{1} \times \frac{2,700}{80}$$

5) A tailor makes a loss of **35%** by selling a suit for **£130**. What was the original cost price? £ _____

b. Finding a % Profit or Loss

Percentage **Profit/Gain or Loss** makes use of exactly the same calculation as percentage increase or decrease.

Finding a Percentage Profit (Appreciation)

Example: Ben bought a computer game for **£12**. He sold it to a friend for **£15**. What was his % profit?

Percentage Profit = $\dfrac{\text{Profit}}{\text{Original Amount}} \times \dfrac{100}{1}$

The extra amount Ben gained was: **£15 – £12 = £3**

Amount ⟶ %

$$\dfrac{^1\cancel{3}}{_1\cancel{12}_{\,4}} \times \dfrac{\cancel{100}^{\,25}}{1} = 25\% \quad \text{\% Profit}$$

Finding a Percentage Loss (Depreciation)

Example: Emily bought an **£8,000** car and sold it later for **£6,600**. What was her % loss?

Percentage Loss = $\dfrac{\text{Loss}}{\text{Original Amount}} \times \dfrac{100}{1}$

The amount Emily lost was: **£8,000 – £6,600 = £1,400**

Amount ⟶ %

$$\dfrac{^7\cancel{1400}}{_{2\,4\,8}\cancel{8000}} \times \dfrac{\cancel{100}^{\,10\,5}}{1} = \dfrac{35}{2} = 17\tfrac{1}{2}\% \quad \text{\% Loss}$$

Exercise 9: 15b   Calculate the following:

6) What is the percentage profit if a computer is bought for **£625** and sold for **£725**? _____ %

Am ⟶ %

$\dfrac{100}{625} \times \dfrac{100}{1}$

7) A man buys a lamp for **£15** and sells it for **£18**. What is his percentage profit? _____ %

Score

8) A greengrocer buys **100** oranges for **£10** and sells them for **14p** each. His percentage profit is _____ %.

9) Nadia bought a ring for **£12.50** and sold it for **£10.25**. Her percentage loss was _____ %.

$$\text{Am} \rightarrow \% \qquad \frac{225}{1250} \times \frac{100}{1}$$

10) Pavendeep bought a mountain bike for **£240** and sold it later for **£180**. What was the percentage loss? _____ %

8. VAT (Value Added Tax)

Value Added Tax (VAT) is a government tax added to various goods and services (exemptions include books and food). It is currently levied at **20%** and is charged at the point of sale of goods or services.

Total cost of goods or services = shop price + 20% VAT

a. Adding VAT to an Amount

Adding VAT (Value Added Tax) **to an Amount** is the same as increasing an amount by a percentage.

Example: A plumber costs a job at **£160** and adds **20%** VAT. How much does he charge the customer?

$$\% \rightarrow \text{Amount}$$

$$\frac{12\cancel{0}}{10\cancel{0}} \times \frac{16\cancel{0}}{1} = 192$$

The plumber charges **£192** (inc. VAT).

Exercise 9: 16a   Calculate the following:

1) A weekend break for a couple costs £260 excluding VAT at 20%. The total cost for a couple is £ _____ .

$$\begin{array}{cc} \% & \rightarrow \text{Am} \\ \dfrac{120}{100} & \times \dfrac{260}{1} \end{array}$$

2) An airline makes a 4% surcharge (extra charge) on a holiday costing £450 to cover extra fuel costs. Find the new price of the holiday. (Treat the 4% surcharge in a similar way to an extra tax like VAT.) £ _____

b. Finding the Cost without VAT

Finding the Cost without VAT uses the same calculation for finding a reverse percentage.

Example: A man buys a television for £282 including VAT at 20%. What is the cost excluding VAT?

$$\% \quad \rightarrow \quad \text{Amount}$$

$$\dfrac{\overset{5}{\cancel{100}}}{1} \times \dfrac{\overset{141}{\cancel{282}}}{\underset{3.6}{\cancel{120}}} = 235$$

The television costs **£235** (excl. VAT).

Exercise 9: 16b   Calculate the following:

3) A personal stereo costs £96 including VAT at 20%. The cost without VAT is £ _____ .

$$\begin{array}{cc} \% & \rightarrow \text{Am} \\ \dfrac{100}{1} & \times \dfrac{96}{120} \end{array}$$

4) A shop offers 5% discount on cash purchases. If a customer paid £152 cash for some goods, what was the original cost price? (Use the reverse % technique.) £ _____

© 2006 Stephen Curran

5) A woman saves **20%** in a sale and buys a coat for **£110**. What was the original price of the coat? £ _____

9. Two Percentages

It can be necessary to follow one percentage by another.

Example: A computer costs **£240** to manufacture. The factory wants **25%** profit and VAT of **20%** must be added. Find the final price.

1. % ⟶ Amount

$$\frac{125}{100} \times \frac{240}{1} = £300$$

2. % ⟶ Amount

$$\frac{120}{100} \times \frac{300}{1} = £360$$

If the final amount is expressed as a percentage it is **not** 25% + 20% = 45% but a percentage increase.

Percentage Increase = $\dfrac{\text{Difference}}{\text{Original Amount}} \times \dfrac{100}{1}$

The extra amount charged: £360 − £240 = £120

Amount ⟶ %   Percentage Increase

$$\frac{120}{240} \times \frac{100}{1} = 50\%$$

Exercise 9: 16c Calculate the following: Score

6-8) A woman gets **10%** off the list price of a **£400** stereo in a sale. If she receives a further discount of **5%** on the sale price for paying cash, what did she pay?

$$\begin{array}{ll} \%\to\text{Am} & \%\to\text{Am} \\ 6)\ \dfrac{90}{100}\times\dfrac{400}{1}=£\underline{\ \ \ \ } & 7)\ \dfrac{95}{100}\times\dfrac{?}{1}=£\underline{\ \ \ \ } \end{array}$$

8) What is the overall percentage decrease?

$$\text{Am}\to\% \qquad \dfrac{?}{400}\times\dfrac{100}{1}=\underline{\ \ \ \ }\%$$

A gas engineer earns **£50** for a job. He receives a **10%** bonus from his firm but pays **20%** tax on the total.

9) Before tax he earns £ _____ .

10) The tax payable is £ _____ .

10. Mixed Percentage Problems

All problems make use of only two types of calculation.

1. Percentage to Amount - Find an amount from a %.

Four kinds of question:
- Basic % to amount.
- Increasing amount by a %.
- Decreasing amount by a %.
- Reverse % (find original amount or 100%).

2. Amount to Percentage - Find a % from an amount.

Three kinds of question:
- Basic amount to %.
- % increase.
- % decrease.

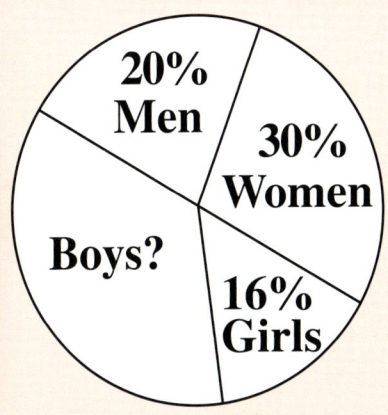

Some questions have to be solved in stages.  Example:

This pie chart shows the proportions of girls, boys, men and women that belong to a tennis club. There are **24** girls in the club. How many boys are there?

1. This is a % to amount. (How many boys are there?)

2. Information given - both halves of the pie chart are **50%**. **16%** represents **24** girls.

3. Information missing.

    a. The % of boys - this can be found by subtraction. $50\% - 16\% = 34\%$

    b. Total number of members in the club.

    i. Find **1%** of the total.   ii. Find **100%**.

    Divide by 2

    Simplify $\cancel{16}\%^{\,6} = \cancel{24}\,^{12}$ girls   Multiply
    $\cancel{8}\% = \cancel{12}$ girls $1\tfrac{1}{2} \times 100 = 150$
    $\cancel{4}\% = \cancel{6}$ girls
    $\cancel{2}\% = \cancel{3}$ girls $100\% = 150$ people
    $1\% = 1\tfrac{1}{2}$ in the club.

4. Calculation.

    $$\frac{\cancel{34}^{\,17}}{\cancel{100}_{\,1}} \times \frac{\cancel{150}^{\,3}}{1} = 51$$

    There are **51** boys in the tennis club.

Exercise 9: 17   Calculate the following:

1) A girl needs **60%** to pass an exam. If there are a possible **250** marks, how many must she score to pass? (% to amount)

    $$\begin{array}{cc} \% & \to \text{Am} \\ \dfrac{60}{100} & \times \dfrac{250}{1} \end{array}$$

    She needs _____ marks to pass.

36

2) A computer game usually costs **£65**. New versions of the game are made **20%** more expensive. (Increase amount by %)

The new version of the game will cost £ _____ .

% → Am

$$\frac{120}{100} \times \frac{65}{1}$$

3) A hamburger meal normally costs **£3.80** but the restaurant is offering **35%** off the normal price. (Decrease amount by %)

% → Am

$$\frac{65}{100} \times \frac{380}{1}$$

The meal will now cost £ _____ .

4) A boy gets **175** out of **250** marks in his maths exam. (Amount to %)

His percentage will be _____ %.

Am → %

$$\frac{175}{250} \times \frac{100}{1}$$

5) A music shop has a sale and reduces its prices on a number of items. A percentage reduction is given for each article with its sale price. What is the original price of each item? (Find the original amount - 100%)

	Items	% Off	Sale Price	Original Price
a)	Videos	15% off	£10.20	£ _____
b)	Tapes	20% off	£2.00	£ _____
c)	CDs	25% off	£10.50	£ _____
d)	Records	35% off	£5.20	£ _____

Example: Question 5) a) Reverse %. Find the percentage sale price first.
100% − 15% = 85%

% → Am

$$\frac{100}{1} \times \frac{1020}{85}$$

6) a) A boy saves **£320** for a CD player but it increases in price to **£400**. What is the percentage increase in price? (% increase)

The percentage increase in price will be _____ %.

$$\frac{Am}{} \rightarrow \% $$
$$\frac{80}{320} \times \frac{100}{1}$$

b) A year later the same boy sells his CD player that he bought for **£400** for **£250**. What did he lose as a percentage? (% decrease)

The percentage loss (decrease) will be _____ %.

$$\frac{Am}{} \rightarrow \%$$
$$\frac{150}{400} \times \frac{100}{1}$$

7) There are **700** animals on a farm.
   a) How many hens are there?

   There are _____ hens.

   b) How many pigs are there?

   There are _____ pigs.

Pigs ?%, Cattle 26%, Hens 31%, Sheep 23%

8) Peter uses **7** of the ice cubes for drinks. What percentage of the cubes are left? Write your answer as a recurring %.

There are _____ % ice cubes left.

9) The new jeans Fiona wants have been reduced by **20%** in a sale. The original price was **£11.50**. How much are they now? The jeans will cost £ _____ .

10) Value Added Tax (VAT) is set at **20%**. A TV set costs **£420**. What will the cost be with VAT? The TV will cost £ _____ .

11. Percentages and Decimals

Percentages are parts of **100** and convert to **Decimals**.

Example: Convert **37%** to a decimal.

Fraction

$$37\% = \frac{37}{100} \rightarrow$$

Put onto the decimal table.

U	t	h	th
0 .	3	7	

a. Changing Percentages to Decimals

Example: Convert **71%** to a decimal.

Divide the percentage by **100**. Move the decimal point two places to the left.

2 places left

$71.0\% \rightarrow 0.71$

Exercise 9: 18a   Convert % to decimal:

1) **14%** = _____   2) **54%** = _____
3) **99%** = _____   4) **150%** = _____
5) **56%** = _____

b. Changing Decimals to Percentages

Example: Convert **0.71** to a percentage.

Multiply the decimal by **100**. Move the decimal point two places to the right.

2 places right

$0.71 \rightarrow 71.0\%$

Exercise 9: 18b Convert decimal to %:

6) **0.94** = _____ % 7) **1.25** = _____ %

8) **0.05** = _____ % 9) **2.65** = _____ %

10) **0.11** = _____ %

c. Percentage-Decimal Calculations

All percentage calculations can be solved using decimals. If numbers do not cancel as fractions, use decimals instead.

(i) Percentage to Amount

A percentage is given and an amount has to be found.

Example: Find **36%** of **250**.

1) Divide **36** by **100**.
   (Move d.p. 2 places left.) $36 \div 100 = 0.36$

2) Multiply **0.36** by **250**.
   (Use long multiplication.) $0.36 \times 250 = 90$

Exercise 9: 19 Find the following amounts:

1) **24%** of **£85**.   2) **13%** of **140km**.
   £ _____   _____ km

3) **16%** of **£224**.   4) **8%** of **30cm**.
   £ _____   _____ cm

5) **72%** of **75 litres**.   6) **15%** of **1.2km**.
   _____ litres   _____ m

7) **2.5%** of **£12**.   8) **7.5%** of **40m**.
   _____ p   _____ m

9) **85%** of **660km**. 10) **1.5%** of **£5**.
   _____ km   _____ p

(ii) Amount to Percentage

An amount is given and a percentage has to be found.

Example: What is **90** as a % of **250**?

1) Divide **90** by **250**. $90 \div 250 = 0.36$
   (Use long division.)

2) Multiply **0.36** by **100**. $0.36 \times 100 = 36\%$
   (Move d.p. 2 places right.)

Exercise 9: 20 Find the following percentages:

1) **24** as a % of **64**.   2) **£7** as a % of **£20**.
   _____ %   _____ %

3) **1200g** as a % of **3kg**.   4) **98mm** as a % of **2.45m**.
   _____ %   _____ %

5) **35m** as a % of **56m**.   6) **4mm** as a % of **3cm**.
   _____ %   _____ %

7) **3.64kg** as a % of **5.6kg**. 8) **60cm** as a % of **4m**.
   _____ %   _____ %

9) **37mm** as a % of **148cm**. 10) **45p** as a % of **£1.35**.
   _____ %   _____ %

© 2006 Stephen Curran

12. Fractions, Decimals and Percentages

a. Useful Equivalents

Fraction	Decimal	Percentage	Fraction	Decimal	Percentage
$\frac{1}{2}$	0.5	50%	$\frac{1}{8}$	0.125	12.5%
$\frac{1}{3}$	$0.\dot{3}$	$33.\dot{3}\%$	$\frac{3}{8}$	0.375	37.5%
$\frac{2}{3}$	$0.\dot{6}$	$66.\dot{6}\%$	$\frac{5}{8}$	0.625	62.5%
$\frac{1}{4}$	0.25	25%	$\frac{7}{8}$	0.875	87.5%
$\frac{3}{4}$	0.75	75%	$\frac{1}{10}$	0.1	10%
$\frac{1}{5}$	0.2	20%	$\frac{1}{100}$	0.01	1%

b. Estimations

This involves **Estimating** fractions, percentages and decimals as proportions of one unit or a whole one.

Example: Estimate the shaded portion as a percentage, decimal and a fraction.

An estimation that is within **5%** of the correct answer is acceptable.

This is approximately:

70% or **0.7** or $\frac{7}{10}$

© 2006 Stephen Curran

Exercise 9: 21

Estimate as a fraction, decimal and percentage:

Score

1)  Fraction = _____

Decimal = _____

Percentage = _____%

2) Fraction = _____

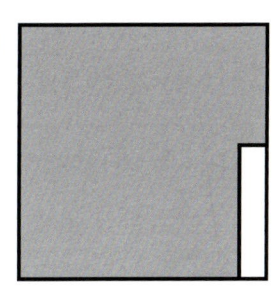

Decimal = _____

Percentage = _____%

3) = _____

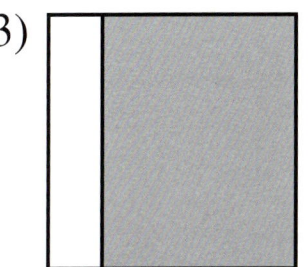

= _____

= _____%

4) = _____

= _____

= _____%

5) = _____

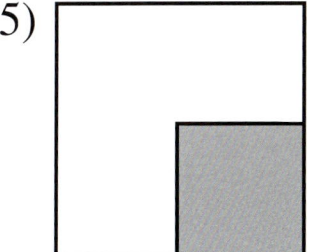

= _____

= _____%

6) = _____

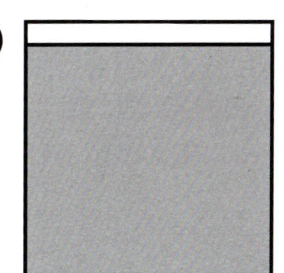

= _____

= _____%

7) = _____

= _____

= _____%

8) = _____

= _____

= _____%

9) = _____

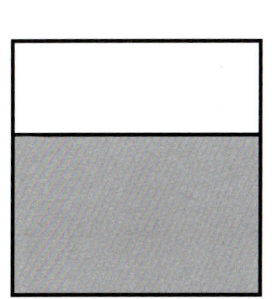

= _____

= _____%

10) = _____

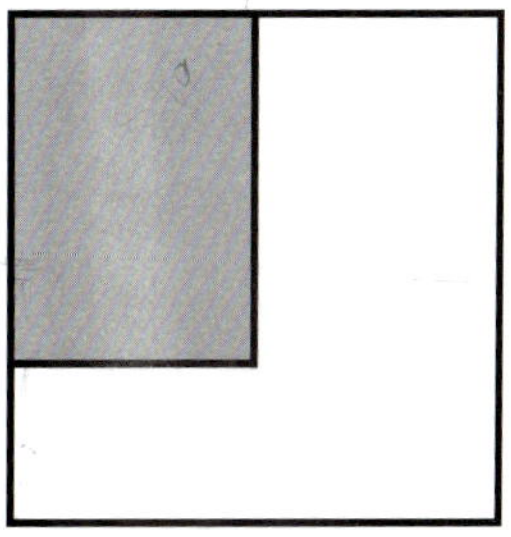

= _____

= _____%

© 2006 Stephen Curran

c. Percentages, Decimals or Fractions

Ordering by size (or magnitude) can be done by changing the parts into **Percentages**, **Decimals or Fractions** depending on what is most convenient.

Example: Put the following in size order, smallest first.

$$\frac{3}{25} \quad 13\% \quad 0.1 \quad 16\% \quad \frac{4}{23}$$

As the LCD is too big (**2300**) it is easier to change them to decimals.

$$\frac{3}{25} \quad 13\% \quad 0.1 \quad 16\% \quad \frac{4}{23}$$

↓ ↓ ↓ ↓ ↓

1. Convert to decimals.   0.12   0.13   0.1   0.16   0.174

↓ ↓ ↓ ↓ ↓

2. Add zeros for comparison.   0.120   0.130   0.100   0.160   0.174

3. Re-order the decimals.   0.100   0.120   0.130   0.160   0.174

↓ ↓ ↓ ↓ ↓

4. Convert to original form.   0.1 $\frac{3}{25}$ 13%   16% $\frac{4}{23}$

Exercise 9: 22   Find the following amounts:

1) Put in size order, smallest first.   4% $\frac{3}{100}$ 0.02   = ___ ___ ___

2) Put in size order, largest first. $\frac{1}{13}$ 0.08   9%   = ___ ___ ___

Which is smallest?

3) 0.1 $\frac{2}{9}$ 2%   ___

4) $\frac{1}{8}$ 0.15   12%   ___

5) $\frac{1}{20}$ 0.06   4%   ___

6) 0.03 $\frac{3}{8}$ 4%   ___

Which is largest?

7) **0.04** $\frac{3}{100}$ **5%** _____

8) **7%** $\frac{1}{12}$ **0.06** _____

9) $\frac{1}{30}$ **0.04** **2%** _____

10) $\frac{1}{11}$ **9%** **0.1** _____

d. Percentage Decimals & Fractions

Percentage Decimals are percentages with a decimal point. Percentages are hundredths of a unit and this must be taken into account when converting a decimal percentage to a normal decimal.

Example: Convert $4\frac{1}{4}$% into a normal decimal.

Percentages are fractions of **100** (parts of a hundred).

The **4 units** of the $4\frac{1}{4}$% are **4 hundredths** : → $\frac{4}{100}$

- Change $\frac{1}{4}$ into **0.25**.
- Divide **4.25** by **100**.   **4.25%** →

U	t	h	th	t/th
0•0		4	2	5

(Move the decimal point 2 places left. If necessary, add zeros to the left of the number, so the point can be moved.)

To change normal decimals into percentage decimals reverse the process - move the decimal point 2 places right.

Exercise 9: 23 Write as normal decimals:

1) **2.13%** = _____

2) **3.6%** = _____

3) **0.7%** = _____

4) **9.89%** = _____

5) $1\frac{4}{5}$% = _____

6) $10\frac{1}{2}$% = _____

Write as percentage decimals:

7) **0.334** = _____

8) **0.069** = _____

9) **0.812** = _____

10) **1.367** = _____

e. Ordering Percentage Decimals

It is important to be able to place **Percentage Decimals** and normal decimals in the correct order of magnitude (size).

Example: Which one of the following is the smallest?

$\frac{1}{25}$ 3.51%   0.05   3.6% $\frac{1}{15}$

3.51%   3.6%   These two amounts have decimal points. Note that percentages are fractions of **100**.

The **3 units** of the % are hundredths:

$\frac{3}{100}$ Divide **3.51** by **100**. 3.51% →

U	t	h	th	t/th
0•0		3	5	1

(Move the decimal point 2 places left.)

Convert the fractions to decimals (see Maths Workbook 2).

1. Convert all the amounts to decimals.

$\frac{1}{25}$ 3.51%   0.05   3.6% $\frac{1}{15}$

↓ ↓ ↓ ↓ ↓

2. Add zeros so it is easier to make comparisons.

0.04   0.0351   0.05   0.036   0.0667

↓ ↓ ↓ ↓ ↓

0.0400   **0.0351**   0.0500   0.0360   0.0667

3.51% is the smallest amount.

Exercise 9: 24 Which is smallest?   Score ____

1) 0.1 $\frac{3}{100}$ 2.15%   ____   2) $\frac{1}{8}$ 0.07   7.1%   ____

3) $\frac{1}{20}$ 0.06   9.9%   ____   4) 0.1 $\frac{3}{8}$ 1.95%   ____

Which is largest?

5) 0.03 $\frac{1}{100}$ 4.16%   ____   6) 7.4% $\frac{1}{12}$ 0.06   ____

7) $\frac{1}{30}$ 0.61%   0.07   ____   8) $\frac{1}{11}$ 9.78%   0.1   ____

9) Put in size order, smallest first.   0.02 $\frac{3}{100}$ 2.1%   = ____ ____ ____

10) Put in size order, largest first. $\frac{1}{13}$ 0.08   9.1%   = ____ ____ ____

© 2006 Stephen Curran

Chapter Ten
RATIO & PROPORTION
1. What is a Ratio?

A **Ratio** is a way of comparing two or more values. The different values are separated by the sign :
This is a colon sign which means either 'compared to' or 'compared with'.
Ratios can be used in two main ways:
    1. To compare one quantity with the whole.
    2. To compare one quantity with another quantity.
Fractions and percentages can also be compared as ratios.

2. Comparing with the Whole

This is where one quantity is compared with the whole. The ratio is written as follows:

    Number of Parts Selected : Total Number of Parts

Example: Hardip has £4. She gives £1 to Tandip. Write this as a ratio compared to the original amount.

Parts Selected : Total Number of Parts
= 1 : 4

a. Ratios and Fractions

A ratio which compares a quantity with a whole can be written as a fraction. The number on the left becomes the numerator and the one on the right becomes the denominator.

Example: **2** out of **5** children have brown hair. Compare the number of children with brown hair with the total number of children. Give your answer as a ratio and as a fraction.

$2 : 5 = \dfrac{2}{5}$

Exercise 10: 1a The following questions involve ratios which compare a quantity with the whole amount. Write the ratio/fraction:

1) a) $\dfrac{4}{5}$ = ___ : ___   b) $\dfrac{1}{2}$ = ___ : ___

2) a) $6 : 7 = \dfrac{}{}$ b) $2 : 19 = \dfrac{}{}$

Score

b. Ratios and Percentages
(i) Ratio to Percentage

A ratio can also be written as a percentage by multiplying the fraction by **100**.

Example: Write one part out of four parts as a percentage.

1. Write as a fraction

   $1 : 4 = \dfrac{1}{4}$

2. Multiply by **100** & simplify

   $\dfrac{1}{\cancel{4}_1} \times \cancel{100}^{25} = \dfrac{25}{1}$

3. Write as a % **25%**

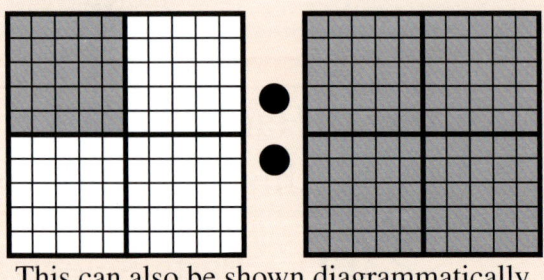

This can also be shown diagrammatically.

Exercise 10: 1b The following ratios compare a quantity with the whole amount. Write them as percentages:

3) $3 : 4 =$ ___%   4) $9 : 20 =$ ___%

5) $13 : 25 =$ ___%   6) $11 : 40 =$ ___%

(ii) Percentage to Ratio

Example: Write **25%** as a ratio which is compared to the whole amount.

1. Convert to a fraction $\dfrac{25}{100}$ 2. Simplify $\dfrac{25}{100}\,{}^{1}_{4}$

3. Express as a ratio **1 : 4**   25% as a ratio = **1 : 4**

Exercise 10: 1c Write the following %s as ratios which compare to the whole amount:

7) **65%** = $\dfrac{65}{100}$ = ___ : ___

8) **90%** = $\dfrac{90}{100}$ = ___ : ___

9) **45%** = ___ : ___

10) **48%** = ___ : ___

3. Comparing with another Quantity

This is where one quantity is compared with another quantity. It is the most common use of ratios. The ratio is written as follows: Number of Parts Selected **:** Number of Parts Not Selected

Example: Hardip has **£4**. She gives **£1** to Tandip. Write the ratio of the amount of money they each have.

Number of Parts Tandip has **:** Number of Parts Hardip has

£1 : £1 £1 £1 = **1 : 3**

a. Ratios and Fractions

Ratios are written as a fraction by dividing both sides by the total number of parts. (Remember to simplify if required.)

Example: **1 compared to 2.** This is written as: **1 : 2**

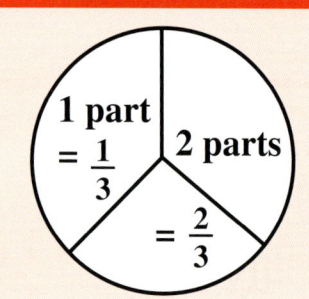

There are three parts in total (**1 + 2**), meaning each part is one third.

1 part to 2 parts   or $\frac{1}{3}$ compared to $\frac{2}{3}$

Exercise 10: 2a

Compare the following quantities as ratios and as fractions:

1) Philip owns **4** CDs and Ann owns **5**.

   ___ : ___

   $\frac{4}{9}$ to ___

2) In a class, **4** out of **11** pupils are boys. The rest are girls.

   Boys : Girls

   ___ : ___

   ___ to ___

3) **11** children keep mice, **5** keep gerbils and **3** keep rabbits.

   ___ : ___ : ___

   ___ to ___ to ___

4) **3** out of **7** girls like netball, the others do not.

   ___ : ___

   ___ to ___

b. Ratios and Percentages

(i) Ratio to Percentage

Ratios comparing quantities can be written as percentages by multiplying the fractions by **100**.

Example: £**50** is shared between **2** children in the ratio **2 : 3**. Write the amounts received by each child as a percentage.

1. Write the ratio as fractions.

   $\frac{2}{5} : \frac{3}{5}$

2. Multiply each fraction by **100**.

   $\frac{2}{5} \times \frac{100}{1} : \frac{3}{5} \times \frac{100}{1}$

3. Cancel each side separately.

   40% : 60%

Exercise 10: 2b Write the following as ratios and percentages:

5) Salima and Cally receive mints in the ratio **3 : 7**. Write their shares as %s.

3 : 7

____% : ____%

6) Anne-Marie has **20** chocolates. She gives **9** to Amanjot. Write their shares as a ratio and as %s.

____ : ____

____% : ____%

(ii) Percentage to Ratio

To write percentages as a ratio, simply insert the **:** and simplify.

Example: £50 is shared between **2** children so that one receives **40%** and the other **60%**. Write the amounts received as a ratio in its simplest form.

1. Write as a ratio.

   40 : 60

2. Simplify.

   $^2\cancel{40} : \cancel{60}^3$ = **2 : 3**

Exercise 10: 2c Write the following percentage shares as ratios:

Score

7) **55% : 45%** = ____ : ____

8) **15% : 30% : 55%** = ____ : ____ : ____

Jaibir wins **80%** of the cash prize in a competition.

9) Write this as a ratio, comparing Jaibir's prize to what he did not win. ____ : ____

10) What would the ratio be if Jaibir had won **85%** of the cash prize? ____ : ____

4. Ratio and Proportion

> A ratio shows the relationship between two quantities. One set of quantities can sometimes be obtained by multiplying each term in another set by a constant multiplier or dividing by a constant divisor. In both these cases, the two sets are said to be in **Direct Proportion**.

Example: Show that the set of quantities **3, 5, 8** is in direct proportion to **12, 20, 32**.

$$\begin{matrix} 3 \\ 5 \\ 8 \end{matrix} \xrightarrow{\times 4} \begin{matrix} 12 \\ 20 \\ 32 \end{matrix} \quad \text{or} \quad \begin{matrix} 3 \\ 5 \\ 8 \end{matrix} \xleftarrow{\div 4} \begin{matrix} 12 \\ 20 \\ 32 \end{matrix}$$

Example: What is the ratio between the two quantities?

The ratio can be obtained by simplifying **3** and **12**.

Divide both quantities by **3**.

$$\cancel{3}^1 \; \cancel{12}^4 \\ 1 : 4$$

Ratios represent amounts. The size of the ratio is in direct proportion to the amounts.

Example: Philip and Jatinda share a paper round in a ratio of **1 : 2** for **18** weeks. Philip does it for **6** weeks and Jatinda **12** weeks.

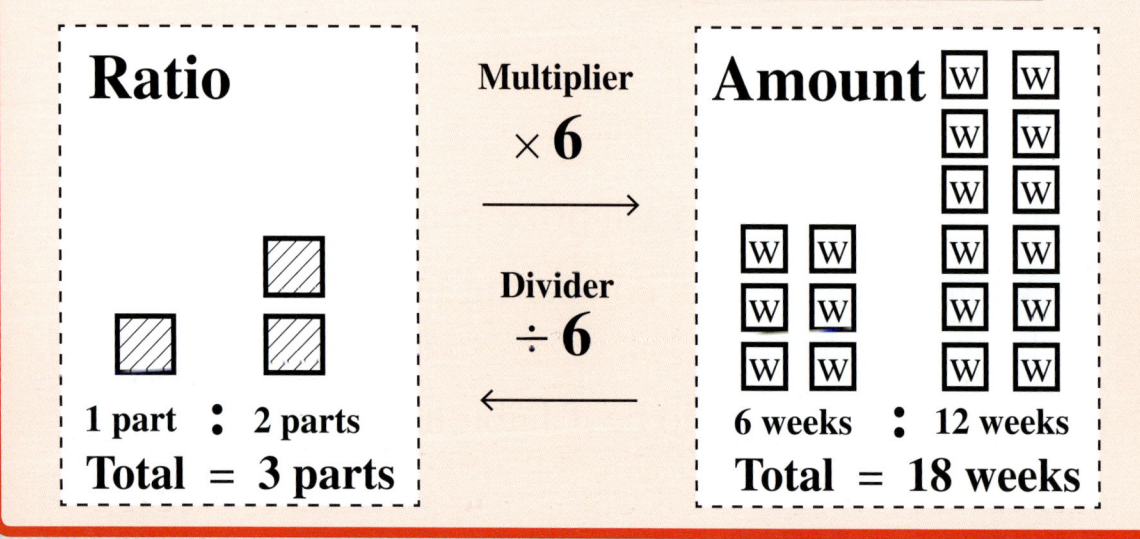

Ratio

1 part : 2 parts
Total = 3 parts

Multiplier
× 6 →

Divider
÷ 6 ←

Amount

6 weeks : 12 weeks
Total = 18 weeks

Ratio Boxes are a way of recording the information given and then calculating whatever is missing.

Total
18
Amounts
6 : 12
Multiplier/Divider ↑   ↑ ×6 ×6 ÷6 ÷6 ↓   ↓
Ratio
1 : 2

The total number of weeks worked by both boys is **6** + **12** = **18** weeks.

Philip has the paper round for **6** weeks. Jatinda has the paper round for **12** weeks.

The ratio can be multiplied by **6** to find the amounts or the amounts can be divided by **6** to find the ratio.

Philip and Jatinda share a paper round in the ratio of **1 : 2**.

The same information can be recorded on a **Fraction Box**. The ratio of **1 : 2** can be converted to fractions:

Fraction given	Fraction given
$\frac{1}{3}$	$\frac{2}{3}$
Amount 1 × 6 = 6	Amount 2 × 6 = 12
6	**12**
Total 6 + 12 = 18 **18**	One part $\frac{1}{3}$ = 6

(See Maths Workbook 2.)

Add the ratio **1 : 2** (1 + 2 = 3). This means there are 3 parts. The ratio can be represented fractionally as:

$\frac{1}{3}$ to $\frac{2}{3}$ is the same as: **1 : 2**

$\frac{1}{3}$ or one part is equal to **6** weeks.

$\frac{1}{3}$ equals **6** weeks (Philip). $\frac{2}{3}$ equals **12** weeks (Jatinda).

The total of 3 parts (**6** + **12**) is equal to **18** weeks.

Ratio and fraction boxes express the same thing in different ways. Confusion is avoided by using fraction boxes to solve fraction problems and ratio boxes to solve ratio problems.

5. Amount to Ratio

This involves expressing the ratio in its simplest form.

Example: Express **45p** and **£1.20** as a ratio in lowest terms.

1. Change to same units (pence).
2. Fill in the ratio box.
3. Simplify/cancel.

The total is not required.

$$\begin{array}{c|c} \text{Amounts} & 45 : 120 \\ \hline \text{Divider} & \div 15 \quad \div 15 \\ \hline \text{Ratio} & 3 : 8 \end{array}$$

$$\cancel{45}^{3\cancel{9}} : \cancel{120}^{8\,\cancel{24}}$$

Divide by **5** then by **3** (or divide by **15**).

$$3 : 8$$

The ratio can also be expressed fractionally as:

$\frac{3}{11}$ to $\frac{8}{11}$ because $3 + 8 = 11$ parts in total.

Exercise 10: 3

Find the ratio and the fractional representation for the amounts:

1) **£5 : £1.75**

$$\begin{array}{c} 500 : 175 \\ \hline \div 25 \quad \div 25 \\ \hline \text{Ratio} \\ \underline{\quad} : \underline{\quad} \end{array}$$

$\frac{20}{27}$ to _____   Fractional representation

2) **150cm : 3.5m**

$$\begin{array}{c} 150 : 350 \\ \hline \\ \hline \underline{\quad} : \underline{\quad} \end{array}$$

_____ to _____

3) **400g : 1.6kg**

[:]
[: ___ ___]

to
___ ___

4) **40cℓ : 1.2ℓ**

[:]
[: ___ ___]

to
___ ___

5) **£36 : £54**

[:]
[: ___ ___]

to
___ ___

6) **1.12m : 56cm**

[:]
[: ___ ___]

to
___ ___

Find the ratio only for the following amounts:

7) **20** girls in a class like orangeade, **6** like cola and **4** like lemonade. What is the ratio?

[: :]
[___ : ___ : ___]

8) A club has **50** people. **30** are men, the others women. What is the ratio?

[:]
[___ : ___]

9) **16** children have a cat, **12** children have a dog and **8** have a hamster. What will the ratio of ownership be between the three kinds of animals?

10) There are **27** horses. **9** are black, **3** are white and the others are brown. What is the ratio between the three different colours of horses?

When ratios are represented as fractions or decimals it is necessary to convert them to whole numbers first.
An extended ratio box can demonstrate the various stages.

If the ratio contains decimals it must be multiplied to convert everything to whole numbers.

Example: Express **3 : 0.25** as a ratio in its simplest form.

Multiply the ratio by **4** to convert it all to whole numbers.

(4 × 3)   (4 × 0.25)

This will not simplify.
12   :   1

Amounts
3 : 0.25
Multiplier
×4   ×4
Ratio
12 : 1

Ratios can be in the form of fractions which means they have to be multiplied first to produce the simplest form.

Example: Express $\frac{2}{3} : \frac{4}{5}$ as a ratio in simplest form.

1. Multiply by the lowest common multiple (LCM) of both fractions.

$\frac{2}{3} \times \frac{15}{1}$ $\frac{4}{5} \times \frac{15}{1}$

(2 × 5)   (4 × 3)

10 : 12

2. Divide (simplify) by the highest common factor (HCF).

Divide by 2   Divide by 2

10 : 12

5 : 6

Amounts
$\frac{2}{3} : \frac{4}{5}$
Multiplier
× 15 × 15
New Amounts
10 : 12
Divider
÷ 2 ÷ 2
Ratio
5 : 6

Exercise 10: 4 Find the ratio from the amounts:

1) $\frac{5}{4} : \frac{5}{7}$

$\frac{5}{4} : \frac{5}{7}$
× 28 × 28
New Amounts
÷ 5 ÷ 5
Ratio ___ : ___

2) $6 : \frac{3}{5}$

$6 : \frac{3}{5}$
× 5 × 5
___ : ___

3) **5 : 0.3̇**

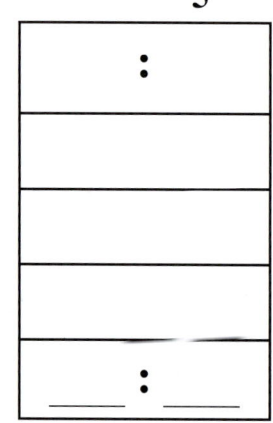

5 : 0.3̇
Multiplier ×3   ×3
Ratio
___ : ___

4) **4/5 : 10**

4/5 : 10
___ : ___

5) **5/7 : 5**

:
___ : ___

6) **0.2 : 4**

0.2 : 4
___ : ___

7) **5/6 : 5/8 : 5/12**

5/6 : 5/8 : 5/12
___ : ___ : ___

8) **3 : 3/5**

:
___ : ___

9) $\frac{3}{4} : 3$

$\frac{3}{4} : 3$
__ : __

10) $2\frac{2}{3} : 1\frac{1}{7}$ Change to improper fractions

Score

:
__ : __

6. Ratio to Amount

There are three types of **Ratio to Amount** questions.
    a. Type 1 - Ratio and Total given.
    b. Type 2 - Ratio and Amount given.
    c. Type 3 - Ratio and Multiplier given.
All three types can be solved with ratio box techniques.

a. Type 1 - (Ratio + Total given)

Example: Sand and cement are mixed in a ratio of **2 : 1**. How much sand and cement is there in a **450kg** mixture?

1. The information given.
   Ratio - **2 : 1**
   Total - **450kg**

2. Place the information into the ratio box.

Total
450kg
Amounts
? : ?
Multiplier
×?   ×?
Ratio
2 : 1

© 2006 Stephen Curran

59

3. Add the ratio.
   2 + 1 = 3

4. Divide the total by 3.
   450 ÷ 3 = 150

5. Multiply the ratio by the multiplier.

   2 × 150 = 300
   1 × 150 = 150

Total
450kg
Amounts
300 : 150
Multiplier
× 150   × 150
Ratio
2 : 1

× ↑ ÷ ↑ +

The mixture is **300kg** of sand and **150kg** of cement.

A shorthand way of remembering the method.

```
Learn the Order of Operations:
    A       D       M
    +   →   ÷   →   ×
```

Exercise 10: 5a   Find the amount:

1) **£120** is won in a draw. It is divided in a ratio of **5 : 7** between two winners. How much did they each receive?

   £ ____ : £ ____

£120
:
5 : 7

2) A fishing line is **18m** long. Divide it in the ratio of **1 : 2 : 3**.

   ____ m : ____ m : ____ m

18m
: :
1 : 2 : 3

60 © 2006 Stephen Curran

b. Type 2 - (Ratio + Amount given)

Example: Billy and Lara save money on a weekly basis in the ratio of **3 : 2**. If Billy saves **£15** a week, how much money does Lara save? How much money do they save altogether?

Total
?
Amounts
15 : ?
Multiplier
× ?   × ?
Ratio
3 : 2

1. The information given.
   Ratio   - **3 : 2**
   Amount - **£15** (Billy)

2. Place the information into the ratio box.

   The multiplier has to be found.

3. Divide amount by **3**.
   $15 \div 3 = 5$

4. Multiply the ratio by the multiplier.
   $2 \times 5 = 10$

5. Add the ratio.
   $15 + 10 = 25$

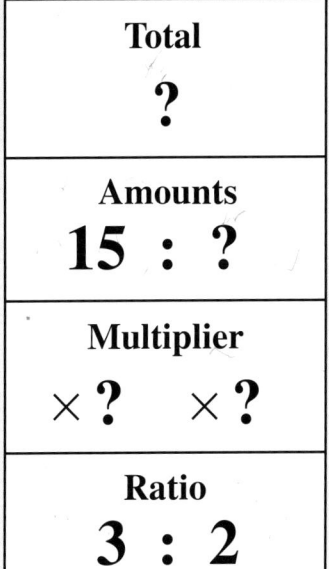

Total
£25
Amounts
15 : **10**
Multiplier
×5   ×5
Ratio
3 : 2

$+$
↑
$\times$
↑
$\div$

Lara saves **£10**. In total they save **£25**.

Learn the Order of Operations:
D   M   A
$\div \rightarrow \times \rightarrow +$

Exercise 10: 5b   Find the amount:

3) A teacher's desk contains pens and pencils in the ratio of **6 : 5**. There are **30** pens. How many pencils are there in the desk? _____ pencils

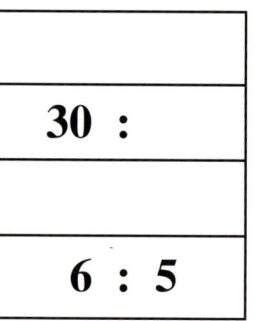

30 :
6 : 5

4) Stephen and Janice share out some stickers in a ratio that can be written fractionally as $\frac{2}{3}$ to $\frac{1}{3}$. Janice receives the larger share of **30**. What share does Stephen receive? _____ stickers

:
:

5) **5** out of every **8** girls in a class like playing netball. If **20** girls like playing netball, how many do not like playing? _____ girls

:
:

c. Type 3 - (Ratio + Multiplier given)

Example: **72** mints were shared among **14** boys and **15** girls (**14 : 15**). If each boy received **3** mints, how many did each girl receive?

Total
72
Amounts
? : ?
Multiplier
×3 ×?
Ratio
14 : 15

1. The information given.
   Ratio   - **14 : 15**
   Multiplier   -   **× 3**

2. Place the information into the ratio box.

The other multiplier has to be found.

3. Multiply the ratio by **3**.
   $3 \times 14 = 42$

4. Subtract the amount from the total.
   $72 - 42 = 30$

5. Divide the amount by the ratio.
   $30 \div 15 = 2$

Total
72
Amounts
42 : 30
Multiplier
×3   ×**2**
Ratio
14 : 15

Each girl receives **2** mints.

Learn the Order of Operations:
M   S   D
× → − → ÷

Exercise 10: 5c Find the missing multiplier:

6) The ratio of wet to dry days during a holiday is **3 : 5**. **Two** children go swimming on every wet day. If **21** children go swimming altogether, how many go swimming on every dry day?

21
:
×2
3 : 5

   _____ children

7) **77** yoyos are owned by one class of children. If **16** children have **two** yoyos each, how many do the other **15** children have each? (The **15** have the same number each.)

   _____ yoyo(s)

© 2006 Stephen Curran

d. Creating the Ratio

Some ratio to amount questions require the creation of the ratio. This is because all that is given is the relationship between the numbers.

Example: | Andy has **half** as many stickers as Billy and Chris has **one third** as many as Billy. Altogether they have **33** stickers. How many does each boy have?

1. Find the ratio.
   Estimate an amount Billy could have, as the other amounts relate to his. It must be a number that is divisible by **2** and by **3**, e.g. **12**.

   Simplify
   Divide by **2**

   Estimate Billy's amount -   ~~12~~ⁿ⁶   **6** stickers
   Andy has half as many -   ~~6~~ ³   **3** stickers
   Chris has one third as many - ~~4~~ ²   **2** stickers

   This gives the ratio **6 : 3 : 2**

2. Find the amount.
   - Add the ratio.
     $6 + 3 + 2 = 11$
   - Divide the total by **11** to find the multiplier.
     $33 \div 11 = 3$
   - Multiply the ratio by the multiplier.

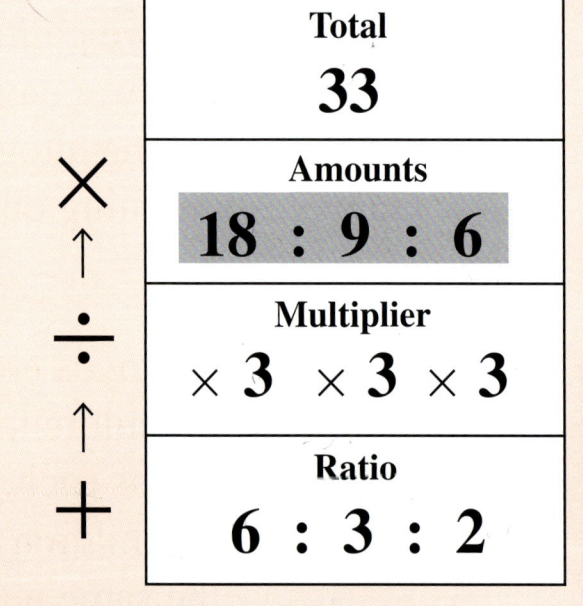

Total
33
Amounts
18 : 9 : 6
Multiplier
× **3** × **3** × **3**
Ratio
6 : 3 : 2

Billy has **18** stickers, Andy has **9** and Chris has **6**.

Exercise 10: 5d Find the amount:

8) The ages of Gran, Auntie and Sue add up to **117**. Gran is **twice** as old as Auntie, who is **4 times** as old as Sue. What are their ages?
Gran ____ Auntie ____ Sue ____

9) An hour (**60mins**) is divided into **3** parts. Part 1 is **twice** as long as part 2, which is **3 times** as long as part 3. How many minutes are in each part?
Part 1 ___ Part 2 ___ Part 3 ___

10) **104** sweets are shared among **3** girls. Paula has **3 times** as many as Jane, who has **3 times** as many as Bavneep. How many does each girl have?
Paula ___ Jane ___ Bavneep ___

7. Other Ratio Types
a. Increasing & Decreasing by Ratio

In these type of questions it is necessary to establish the relationship between one unit and the larger amount.

Example: **Seven** men take **28** days to build a house. How long would it take **4** men?

1. Multiply to find out how long it would take for **one** man to build the house. It would take **seven times** as long. $7 \times 28 = 196$ days for **one** man to build the house.

2. Divide to find out how long it would take **4** men to build the house.   **196 ÷ 4 = 49 days**

It would take **49** days for **4** men to build the house.

Exercise 10: 6a   Find the amount:

1) If **8** children can plant a garden with seeds in **10** hours, how long would it take **20** children to do the same job? (Assume they work at the same speed.) _____ hours

2) If **5** people were hired to clean an office building it would take **18** days. How long would it take just **3** people to do the same job? _____ days

b. Unequal Shares

This type occurs when quantities are not divided into equal parts or shares. Questions often contain the words 'greater than', 'more than', 'less than' or 'fewer than'. The first kind of question has two **Unequal Shares**:

Example:
> In one season Arsenal and Chelsea scored a total of **190** goals. Chelsea scored **40** goals fewer than Arsenal. How many goals did each team score?

1. Subtract the difference between the two quantities from the total quantity.   **190 − 40 = 150 goals**
2. Divide the answer by **2**. This gives the smaller amount.
   150 ÷ 2 = Chelsea scored 75 goals
3. Add the difference in amounts to find the larger amount.
   75 + 40 = Arsenal scored 115 goals

> **Order of Operations is Subtract ⟶ Divide ⟶ Add**

Exercise 10: 6b Find the amount:

3) Vidhur and Anne together have a total of **£10.60**. Vidhur has **£2.40** more than Anne. How much does each child have?

Subtract _____ − _____ = _____
Divide _____ ÷ **2** = _____ (Anne's share)
Add _____ + _____ = _____ (Vidhur's share)
Vidhur has £ _____ and Anne has £ _____ .

4) The sum of two numbers is **420**. The difference between the two numbers is **60**. What are the two numbers?
The smaller number is ____ . The bigger number is ____ .

5) A piece of string **130cm** long is cut into two different lengths. One piece is **50cm** longer than the other. What is the length of each piece of string?
The short piece is _____ cm. The long piece is _____ cm.

Some questions involve repeating the process twice. This second kind of question has three unequal shares:

Example: Pauline and Katherine together have **£40** more than Julie. Pauline has **£8** more than Katherine. If they have **£480** altogether, how much do they each have?

Stage One - If Pauline and Katherine are grouped as one person it is then possible to work out how much Julie has.

1. Subtract the difference in amounts between Pauline/Katherine and Julie (**£40**) from the whole amount (**£480**).

£480 − £40 = £440

2. Divide the answer by **2**. This gives the smaller amount.

£440 ÷ 2 = Julie's share is £220

3. Add the difference in amounts (**£40**) to Julie's share (**£220**) to find Pauline/Katherine's share (larger amount).

$$£220 + £40 = \text{Pauline/Katherine's share of } £260$$

Stage Two - Pauline and Katherine's share (**£260**) now has to be separated. The same stages now have to be repeated. Pauline has **£8** more than Katherine.

4. Subtract the difference in amounts between Pauline and Katherine (**£8**) from the whole amount (**£260**).

$$£260 - £8 = £252$$

5. Divide the answer by **2**. This gives the smaller amount.

$$£252 \div 2 = \text{Katherine's share of } £126$$

6. Add the difference in amounts (**£8**) to Katherine's share (**£126**) to find Pauline's share (larger amount).

$$£126 + £8 = \text{Pauline's share of } £134$$

Answer - The **£480** is shared out in the following ways: Julie has **£220**; Katherine has **£126**; Pauline has **£134**.

Order of Operations   **Subtract → Divide → Add**
was repeated twice over.   **Subtract → Divide → Add**

Exercise 10: 6c   Find the amount:

6) **Three** boys did a sponsored walk and raised **£660** for a local charity. Alex and Dean raised **£240** more than John. Alex raised **£60** more than Dean. How much did they each raise?

Stage One - To find John's share treat Alex/Dean as one.

Subtract   ____ − ____ = ____

Divide   ____ ÷ 2 = ____ (John's share)

Add   ____ + ____ = ____ (Alex/Dean's share)

68 © 2006 Stephen Curran

Stage Two - Now it is time to find Alex and Dean's share.

Subtract   _____ − _____ = _____
Divide   _____ ÷ **2** = _____ (Dean's share)
Add   _____ + _____ = _____ (Alex's share)
John raised £ _____ ; Alex raised £ _____ ; Dean raised £ _____ .

7) Daniel, Premdeep and Ravi altogether have collected **600** stamps. Daniel and Premdeep together have **120** more stamps than Ravi. Daniel has **48** stamps more than Premdeep. How many stamps does each child have?
Ravi has _____ ; Daniel has _____ ; Premdeep has _____ .

c. Double Shares

Some sharing questions have an amount that has been counted twice.

Example: | Sam and Priya together have **£48**. Sam and Carl together have **£64**. Altogether the **three** children have **£84**. Work out how much each child has.

Notice that there are **four** amounts but only **three** children. Sam's amount has been counted twice.

1. Add the Sam/Priya (**£48**) and Sam/Carl (**£64**) amounts.
   £48 + £64 = £112 (Sam's share has been counted twice.)

2. Subtract the total amount (**£84**) from the above (**£112**).
   £112 − £84 = £28 (This gives Sam's share.)

Sam's share can now be used to find the other shares:

3. Subtract Sam's (**£28**) from Sam/Priya's (**£48**) amounts.
   £48 − £28 = £20 (This gives Priya's share.)

4. Subtract Sam's (**£28**) from Sam/Carl's (**£64**) amounts.
   £64 − £28 = £36 (This gives Carl's share.)

Answer - Sam has **£28**; Priya has **£20**; Carl has **£36**.

Exercise 10: 6d Find the amount:

8) James and Keshav together have **92** swap cards. James and Andrew together have **72** swap cards. Altogether the **three** boys have **126** swap cards.

   a) Who has the least swap cards? _____
   b) Who has the most swap cards? _____

   Keshav gives some of his swap cards to the other **two** boys, so they all have the same number (divide total by **3**).

   c) How many did he give to James? _____ swap cards
   d) How many did he give to Andrew? _____ swap cards

9) Melanie buys **6** erasers and **8** pencils at a cost of **£3.40**. Julie buys **6** erasers and **4** pencils at a cost of **£2.60**. In all they spend **£6.00**. (Clue - find cost of **1** pencil & **1** eraser.)
   Use this information to find the cost of:

   a) **6** pencils. £ _____   b) **3** erasers + **2** pencils. £ _____

d. More Complex Ratio Problems

Some ratio box questions can seem more complicated:

Example: Vicky and Wendy collected **four times** as much waste paper as Betty. Vicky collected **16kg** more than Wendy. Altogether they collected **240kg**. How much did each girl collect?

Total
240
Amounts
192 : 48
Multiplier
×48 ×48
Ratio
4 : 1

1. For a ratio, group Vicky and Wendy:

   4 : 1
   Vicky/Wendy   Betty

   This part of the question follows the standard ratio box format.

   The order of operations is: + → ÷ → ×

Therefore Vicky/Wendy collected **192kg** and Betty collected **48kg**.

We also know Vicky collected **16kg** more than Wendy. So, use either the Subtract, Divide, Add method (pp. 66-69) or the following steps:

2. Divide Vicky/Wendy's share by **2**.   **192kg ÷ 2 = 96kg**
3. Add/subtract to Vicky/Wendy's shares to create a gap of **16kg**. Add **8kg** to Vicky's share; Subtract **8kg** from Wendy's share.

Vicky	Wendy
96kg	**96kg**
+ 8	− 8
104kg	**88kg**

Vicky has **104kg**; Wendy has **88kg**; Betty has **48kg**.

Exercise 10: 6e   Find the amount:

Score

10) Paul, John and Don together have **252** stickers. John receives **6** from Paul, and Don gives **4** to John. At the end they discover that Paul has **twice** as many as John and John has **twice** as many as Don.

Create the ratio and use the ratio box to find the final amounts.
a) At the finish Paul has _____, John has _____, Don has _____.
Reverse what was given/taken to each to find the original amounts.
b) At the start Paul has _____, John has _____, Don has _____.

8. Maps and Scale Drawings

Ratios are used for **Maps and Scale Drawings**. The ratio is in direct proportion to the actual distance represented.

Example: A map scale reads **1cm : 3km**. If a distance on the map measures **5cm**, the real distance will be **15km**.

Amounts
5 : 15

Multiplier/Divider
×5   ×5
÷5   ÷5

Scale
1 : 3

© 2006 Stephen Curran

a. Amount to Scale

Example:

A school hall is **40m** long. If a plan represents this as **8cm**, what is the scale?

Amounts
8cm : 40m
Divider
? ?
Scale
? : ?

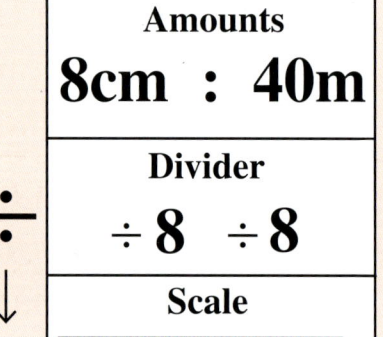

1. Fill in the ratio box.
2. Divide the amounts by a factor of both amounts.

$8 \div 8 = 1$

$40 \div 8 = 5$

The scale is **1cm : 5m**

Amounts
8cm : 40m
Divider
÷8 ÷8
Scale
1cm : 5m

This is best expressed using the same units. This gives **1cm : 500cm** or simply **1 : 500**

Exercise 10: 7a   Write the scale:

1) a) A plan is drawn for a bird table. The bird table measures **20cm** on the plan. What scale has been used?

The scale is ___ : ___

1.8m

b) A class of year 5 children do some orienteering. Their journey of **49.5km** measures **16.5cm** on the map. What is the scale of the map? ___ cm : ___ km
Convert the ratio to cm. ___ : ___

c) A scale drawing is made of a wardrobe. The height of the wardrobe on the drawing measures **9cm** and the real height is **180cm**. The scale is ___ : ___

b. Scale to Amount

Example:

On a plan a school hall is drawn at a scale of **1cm** to **5m**. What is the real length?

School Hall
← 8cm →

| Amounts |
| 8cm : ? |
| Multiplier |
| ? ? |
| Scale |
| 1cm : 5m |

1. Fill in the ratio box.
2. Divide the amount by the scale to find the multiplier.
   $8 \div 1 = 8$
3. Multiply the ratio by the multiplier.
   $5 \times 8 = 40m$

The real length of the hall is **40m**.

| Amounts |
| 8cm : 40m |
| Multiplier |
| × 8 × 8 |
| Scale |
| 1cm : 5m |
| (1 : 500) |

× ↑ ÷

Exercise 10: 7b   Find the amount:

2) a) A new running track is built to a scale of **1cm : 250m**. What is the actual distance **once** round the track?
The distance is _____ m.

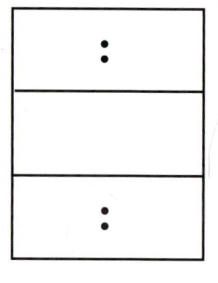

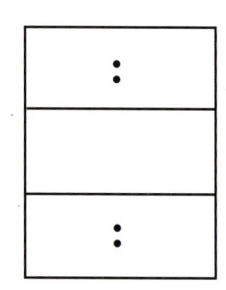

Distance once round on the plan is **6cm**.

b) A path is being laid in a garden. The path is **12m** long. A plan was drawn using a scale of **0.2cm : 1m**. What does the path measure on the plan?
It measures _____ cm.

c) 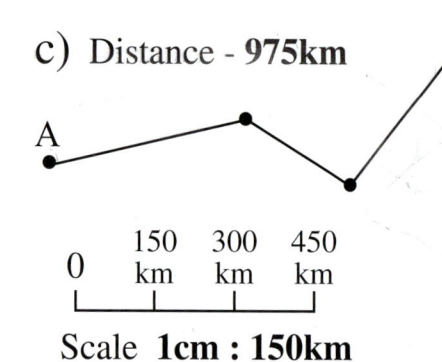 Distance - 975km

Scale **1cm : 150km**

B) An aircraft flies from point A to point B. What does this measure on the map?
It measures _____ cm.

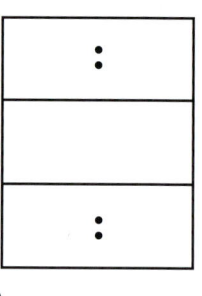

c. Expressing Scales as 1 : n

Sometimes it may be necessary to write a scale in the form **1 : n**. This allows different scales to be compared with one another. Ordinance Survey maps are written in this format. **n** stands for a number that has to be worked out.

Example: Express the scale **4cm : 3.5m** in the form **1 : n**.

1. Convert the ratio so it uses the same units on both sides.

$$3.5m = 3.5 \times 100 = 350cm$$
$$4cm : 3.5m = 4cm : 350cm$$

2. Since the units are now the same, they can be left out, giving **4 : 350**

3. Now divide both sides by the first number:

$$4 \div 4 = 1$$
$$350 \div 4 = 87.5$$

Therefore **4cm : 3.5m** written in the form **1 : n** becomes

1 : 87.5

It can also be done using a ratio box.

Amounts
4 : 350
Divider
÷ 4   ÷ 4
Scale
1 : 87.5

Exercise 10: 7c

Write the following scales in the form **1 : n**:

3) a) **2m : 3m = 1 : ____**

2 : 3
1 :

b) **4cm : 5m = 1 : ____**

4 : 500
1 :

4) a) **3m : 45m = ____ : ____**   b) **2cm : 2½cm = ____ : ____**

5) **5cm : 3.1m = ____ : ____**   6) **6mm : 5.1cm = ____ : ____**

7) **12m : 1.86km = ____ : ____**   8) **17cm : 2.55m = ____ : ____**

d. More Complex Scale Problems

Scales sometimes require conversion from km to cm.

Example: A map of Wales is drawn to a scale of **1 : 650,000**. What would a distance of **130km** be in centimetres on the map?

The scale is in centimetres. It needs to show cm to km.

1cm : 650,000c̶m̶ m → 1cm : 6.500m̶ km

Convert to metres
Divide by **100** (move the decimal point two places to the left - **100cm** to **1m**). (For Metric Conversions see Maths Workbook 2.)

Convert to kilometres
Divide by **1000** (move the decimal point three more places to the left - **1000m** to **1km**).

For speedy conversions it is useful to know there are **100,000cm** in **1km**. In other words move the d.p. 5 places left.

The scale is **1cm : 6.5km**

1. Fill in the ratio box.

2. Divide the amount by the scale to find the multiplier.

   130cm ÷ 6.5cm = 20

3. Multiply the scale by the multiplier.

   1cm × 20 = 20cm

130km will be **20cm** on the map.

Amounts
? : 130km
Multiplier
?   ?
Scale
1cm : 6.5km

Amounts
20cm : 130km
×20   ×20
Scale
1cm : 6.5km

× ↑
÷

Exercise 10: 7d   Calculate the following:

9) a) A map of Great Britain is drawn to a scale of **1 : 800,000**.

   What real distance is represented by **1cm** on the map?

   Cancel
   ↓
   1 : 800,000

   1cm = _____ km

76   © 2006 Stephen Curran

b) A map of Sweden is drawn to a scale of **3 : 750,000**.

What real distance is represented by **1cm** on the map?

Cancel
↓
3 : 750,000

1cm = ____ km

10) a) A map of Scotland is drawn to a scale of **1 : 300,000**.

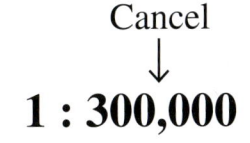

Cancel
↓
1 : 300,000

1cm = ____ km

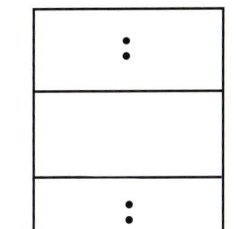

How would **24km** be represented on the map? _____ cm

b) A map of Brazil is drawn to a scale of **5 : 400,000**.

Cancel
↓
5 : 400,000

1cm = ____ km

c) What real distance would **10cm** on the map represent? _____ km

Score

9. Gradients

Gradient is a way of measuring a slope. For every **1 unit** this slope rises on the Vertical Plane, it extends for **5 units** on the Horizontal Plane.

1 unit

5 units

It can be expressed as:

A Ratio
Vertical   Horizontal
(Rise)   (Distance)
 1   :   5

A Percentage
• Change the ratio to a fraction
• Multiply by 100
• Simplify

$$\frac{1}{\cancel{5}_1} \times \frac{\cancel{100}^{20}}{1} = 20\%$$

This is the same as 'comparing with the whole' (p.47 onwards).

© 2006 Stephen Curran

a. Amount to Gradient

Example: A forklift truck rises **5m** travelling up a **50m** ramp. What is the gradient?

1. Find the HCF of **50** and **5**. It is **5**.
2. Cancel the amounts (divide by **5**).
3. To express as a percentage.
   - Change gradient to fraction.
   - Multiply by **100** and cancel.
   - Write as a %.

Amounts	
Rise	Distance
5 : 50
Divider	
÷5	÷5
Gradient	
1 : 10

$$\frac{1}{{}^1\cancel{10}} \times \frac{\cancel{100}^{10}}{1}$$

The gradient is **1 : 10** or **10%**

Exercise 10: 8a   Write the gradient:

1) A car travels **126** metres up a hill. The height of the hill is **28** metres. What is the gradient as a ratio?

   The gradient is ___ : ___

2) A mountain track rises **18** metres over a length of **72** metres. What is the gradient as a ratio and percentage?

   The gradient is ___ : ___   ___%

3) Tom climbs up a steep hill for **160** metres. The height of the hill is **80** metres. Write the gradient as a ratio and percentage.

   The gradient is ___ : ___   ___%

b. Gradient to Amount

Finding amounts can involve calculating either the rise or the distance by using the gradient.

Example: An athlete runs uphill. He covers a horizontal distance of **400m**. The gradient is **1 : 5 (20%)**. What is the rise?

1. If the gradient is given as a percentage, then convert to a ratio.
   - Change to a fraction
   - Simplify/cancel
   - Express fraction as a ratio

   $$\frac{20}{100} = \frac{1}{5}$$

   1 : 5

2. Divide the distance by the gradient to find the multiplier.
   $400 \div 5 = 80$

3. Multiply the gradient by the multiplier.
   $1 \times 80 = 80$

| Amounts | |
Rise	Distance
80m	**400m**
Multiplier	
× 80	× 80
Gradient	
1	5

The rise (height) is **80m**.

Exercise 10: 8b   Write the rise/distance:

4) A mountaineer climbs uphill for **300m**. The gradient is **2 : 3**. What is the rise?

   The rise (height) is _____ m.

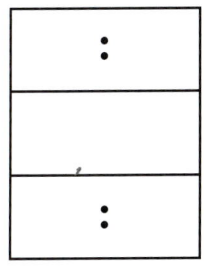

5) A ski-lift rises **315m**. The gradient is **15 : 4**. What distance does the ski-lift cover?

   The distance is _____ m.

6) A train travels **875km**. The gradient is **2%**. What is the rise?

Convert 2% to a ratio. $\dfrac{2}{100} =$

The rise is _____ km.

7) A window cleaner climbs a ladder. The rise is **12m**. The gradient is **6 : 1**. What distance does the foot of the ladder measure from the wall of the house?

The distance is _____ m.

8) Some climbers ascend a mountain. The gradient is **15 : 2**. The climbers ascend to a height of **225m**.

The distance is _____ m.

9) Some children ski down a slope. The distance is **925m**. The gradient is **8%**. What is the rise of the slope?

Convert 8% to a ratio. $\dfrac{8}{100} =$

The rise is _____ m.

10) Some scouts go on an expedition. They walk a distance of **48km** at a gradient of **1 : 6**. What is the rise?

The rise is _____ km.

Score

10. Mixed Ratio Problems

Exercise 10: 9 Calculate the following:

1) 96 marbles are shared between **2** children in the ratio **11 : 5**. How many marbles does each child receive?

   _____ and _____ marbles

96
:
11 : 5

2) Aaron eats **45%** of the chocolate he is given by his mother. Write this as a ratio, comparing the chocolates consumed with the total number Aaron was given. Simplify your answer.

   _____ : _____

3) The ratio of boys to girls in a class is **5 : 4**. If there are **12** girls, how many children are there altogether? _____ children

4) A cake is split into **18** small slices. If Alex receives **half** the number of slices as Ben, who receives a **third** as many as Colin, how many slices of cake does each child receive?

   Alex receives _____ slices.
   Ben receives _____ slices.
   Colin receives _____ slices.

:
:

5) A map of Mexico is drawn to a scale of **3 : 1,100,000**. How would **16.5km** be represented on the map?
   _____ cm

6) A mountaineer climbs up a steep mountain. The gradient is **25 : 3**. If he ascends to a height of **187.5m**, what horizontal distance does he cover?

_____ m

7) **46** stickers are shared among **six** girls and **seven** boys. If each girl receives **3** stickers, how many does each boy receive?

_____ stickers

8) A map of Spain is drawn to a scale of **5 : 1,000,000**. What real distance is represented by **22.5cm**?

_____ km

9) If **9** men can build a house in **18** months, how many years and months would it take for **6** men to build the same house? (Assume they all work at the same speed.)

_____ yrs _____ months

10) **470** stickers are shared between Roger, Sam and Tony. Roger and Sam together have **60** more stickers than Tony. Sam has **25** fewer stickers than Roger.

a) How many stickers does Tony have?

_____ stickers

b) How many more stickers does Tony have than Sam?

_____ stickers   Score

Answers

11+ Maths
Year 5-7 Workbook 3

Chapter Nine
Percentages

Exercise 9: 1
1) 42%
2) 24%
3) 48%
4) 45%
5) Shade 32 squares
6) Shade 23 squares
7) Shade 12 squares
8) Shade 55 squares
9) 20%
10) Check yourself

Exercise 9: 2
1) $6/25$
2) $4/5$
3) $7/20$
4) $19/20$
5) $3/5$
6) $1/1$ or 1
7) $4/25$
8) $2/5$
9) $39/100$
10) $18/25$

Exercise 9: 3
1) $1\frac{1}{2}$
2) $3\frac{1}{5}$
3) $3\frac{7}{10}$
4) $5/1$ or 5
5) $2\frac{1}{10}$
6) $1\frac{6}{25}$
7) $3\frac{3}{20}$
8) $6\frac{3}{4}$
9) $1\frac{1}{20}$
10) $4\frac{3}{5}$

Exercise 9: 4
1) $1/30$
2) $3/8$
3) $2/3$
4) $1/6$
5) $7/8$
6) $1/16$
7) $5/8$
8) $1/12$
9) $5/6$
10) $1/15$

Exercise 9: 5
1) 80%
2) 90%
3) 36%
4) 65%
5) 40%
6) 70%
7) 95%
8) 18%
9) 30%
10) 68%

Exercise 9: 6
1) 160%
2) 370%
3) 450%
4) 345%
5) 168%
6) 225%
7) 105%
8) 112%
9) 330%
10) 220%

Exercise 9: 7
1) $31\frac{1}{4}$%
2) $16\frac{2}{3}$%
3) $58\frac{1}{3}$%
4) $87\frac{1}{2}$%
5) $73\frac{1}{3}$%
6) $83\frac{1}{3}$%
7) $6\frac{2}{3}$%
8) $41\frac{2}{3}$%
9) $37\frac{1}{2}$%
10) $93\frac{1}{3}$%

Exercise 9: 8
1) 8
2) 6
3) 170
4) 450
5) 168
6) 7.2g
7) £1.69
8) £11.20
9) 13.5m
10) £5.70

Exercise 9: 9a
1) £2.88
2) £500
3) 21cm
4) 39km

Exercise 9: 9b
5) 663g
6) £262.50

Exercise 9: 9c
7) 8p
8) £5
9) 90cm
10) 15km

Exercise 9: 10a
1) £1.08
2) £32.50
3) 225cm
4) 22km
5) 525m

Exercise 9: 10b
6) 48p
7) £28
8) 78cm
9) 13km
10) 91m

Exercise 9: 11
1) 250
2) 820
3) £240
4) 300km
5) £4.75
6) 260cm
7) 160m
8) £70
9) 350g
10) 60p

Exercise 9: 12a
1) 15%
2) 17%
3) 36%
4) 20%

Exercise 9: 12b
5) 350%
6) 250%

Exercise 9: 12c
7) $43\frac{3}{4}$%
8) $41\frac{2}{3}$%
9) $37\frac{1}{2}$%
10) $83\frac{1}{3}$%

Exercise 9: 13
1) 62.5%
2) 80%
3) 20%
4) 96.25%
5) 30%
6) 20%
7) 20%
8) 25%
9) 37.5%
10) 85%

Exercise 9: 14
1) £1.82
2) 42cm
3) 45km
4) £2.61
5) £1.54
6) 950km
7) 36%
8) 12.5%
9) 37.5%
10) 25%

11+ Maths
Year 5-7 Workbook 3

Answers

Exercise 9: 15a
1) £120   2) £2,500
3) £15   4) £3,375
5) £200

Exercise 9: 15b
6) 16%   7) 20%
8) 40%   9) 18%
10) 25%

Exercise 9: 16a
1) £312   2) £468

Exercise 9: 16b
3) £80   4) £160
5) £137.50

Exercise 9: 16c
6) £360   7) £342
8) 14.5% 9) £55
10) £11

Exercise 9: 17
1) 150 marks
2) £78
3) £2.47
4) 70%
5) a) £12
   b) £2.50
   c) £14
   d) £8
6) a) 25%
   b) 37.5%
7) a) 217 hens
   b) 140 pigs
8) 41.$\dot{6}$%
9) £9.20
10) £504

Exercise 9: 18a
1) 0.14   2) 0.54
3) 0.99   4) 1.5
5) 0.56

Exercise 9: 18b
6) 94%   7) 125%
8) 5%   9) 265%
10) 11%

Exercise 9: 19
1) £20.40 2) 18.2km
3) £35.84 4) 2.4cm
5) 54 litres 6) 180m
7) 30p   8) 3m
9) 561km 10) 7.5p

Exercise 9: 20
1) 37.5% 2) 35%
3) 40%   4) 4%
5) 62.5% 6) 13.$\dot{3}$%
7) 65%   8) 15%
9) 2.5%   10) 33.$\dot{3}$%

Exercise 9: 21
Answers should be within 0.05 or 5% of the answers given below.
1) $^1/_3$ 0.$\dot{3}$ 33.$\dot{3}$%
2) $^{19}/_{20}$ 0.95 95%
3) $^4/_5$ 0.8 80%
4) $^2/_5$ 0.4 40%
5) $^1/_4$ 0.25 25%
6) $^9/_{10}$ 0.9 90%
7) $^1/_8$ 0.125 12.5%
8) $^4/_5$ 0.8 80%
9) $^5/_8$ 0.625 62.5%
10) $^1/_3$ 0.$\dot{3}$ 33.$\dot{3}$%

Exercise 9: 22
1) 0.02 $^3/_{100}$ 4%
2) 9% 0.08 $^1/_{13}$
3) 2%
4) 12%
5) 4%
6) 0.03
7) 5%
8) $^1/_{12}$
9) 0.04
10) 0.1

Exercise 9: 23
1) 0.0213 2) 0.036
3) 0.007   4) 0.0989
5) 0.018   6) 0.105
7) 33.4%   8) 6.9%
9) 81.2%   10) 136.7%

Exercise 9: 24
1) 2.15%
2) 0.07
3) $^1/_{20}$
4) 1.95%
5) 4.16%
6) $^1/_{12}$
7) 0.07
8) 0.1
9) 0.02 2.1% $^3/_{100}$
10) 9.1% 0.08 $^1/_{13}$

Chapter Ten
Ratio and Proportion

Exercise 10: 1a
1) a) 4 : 5 b) 1 : 2
2) a) $^6/_7$ b) $^2/_{19}$

Exercise 10: 1b
3) 75%   4) 45%
5) 52%   6) 27.5%

Exercise 10: 1c
7) 13 : 20 8) 9 : 10
9) 9 : 20   10) 12 : 25

Exercise 10: 2a
1) 4 : 5 $^4/_9$ to $^5/_9$
2) 4 : 7 $^4/_{11}$ to $^7/_{11}$

84

© 2006 Stephen Curran

Answers

11+ Maths
Year 5-7 Workbook 3

3) 11 : 5 : 3
$^{11}/_{19}$ to $^{5}/_{19}$ to $^{3}/_{19}$
4) 3 : 4 $^{3}/_{7}$ to $^{4}/_{7}$

Exercise 10: 2b
5) 30% : 70%
6) 11 : 9 or 9 : 11
55% : 45% or
45% : 55%

Exercise 10: 2c
7) 11 : 9   8) 3 : 6 : 11
9) 4 : 1   10) 17 : 3

Exercise 10: 3
1) 20 : 7 and $^{20}/_{27}$ to $^{7}/_{27}$
2) 3 : 7 and $^{3}/_{10}$ to $^{7}/_{10}$
3) 1 : 4 and $^{1}/_{5}$ to $^{4}/_{5}$
4) 1 : 3 and $^{1}/_{4}$ to $^{3}/_{4}$
5) 2 : 3 and $^{2}/_{5}$ to $^{3}/_{5}$
6) 2 : 1 and $^{2}/_{3}$ to $^{1}/_{3}$
7) 10 : 3 : 2
8) 3 : 2
9) 4 : 3 : 2
10) 3 : 1 : 5

Exercise 10: 4
1) 7 : 4   2) 10 : 1
3) 15 : 1   4) 2 : 25
5) 1 : 7   6) 1 : 20
7) 4 : 3 : 2   8) 5 : 1
9) 1 : 4   10) 7 : 3

Exercise 10: 5a
1) £50 : £70
2) 3m : 6m : 9m

Exercise 10: 5b
3) 25 pencils
4) 15 stickers
5) 12 girls

Exercise 10: 5c
6) 3 children
7) 3 yoyos

Exercise 10: 5d
8) 72 : 36 : 9 years
9) 36 : 18 : 6 minutes
10) 72 : 24 : 8 sweets

Exercise 10: 6a
1) 4 hours
2) 30 days

Exercise 10: 6b
3) Vidhur has £6.50
   Anne has £4.10
4) Smaller number is 180
   Bigger number is 240
5) Shorter piece is 40cm
   Longer piece is 90cm

Exercise 10: 6c
6) John has £210
   Alex has £255
   Dean has £195
7) Ravi has 240
   Daniel has 204
   Premdeep has 156

Exercise 10: 6d
8) a) Andrew has least
   b) Keshav has most
   c) He gives 4 to James
   d) He gives 8 to Andrew
9) a) £1.20 b) £1.30

Exercise 10: 6e
10) a) At the finish Paul has 144, John has 72 and Don has 36.
    b) At the start Paul has 150, John has 62 and Don has 40.

Exercise 10: 7a
1) a) 1 : 9
   b) 1cm : 3km
      1cm : 300,000cm
   c) 1 : 20

Exercise 10: 7b
2) a) 1500m
   b) 2.4cm
   c) 6.5cm

Exercise 10: 7c
3) a) $1^{1}/_{2}$ or 1.5
   b) 125
4) a) 1 : 15
   b) 1 : $1^{1}/_{4}$ or 1 : 1.25
5) 1 : 62
6) 1 : 8.5 or 1 : $8^{1}/_{2}$
7) 1 : 155
8) 1 : 15

Exercise 10: 7d
9) a) 8km   b) 2.5km
10) a) 8cm   b) 0.8km
    c) 8km

Exercise 10: 8a
1) 2 : 9 or 1 : 4.5
2) 1 : 4 & 25%
3) 1 : 2 and 50%

Exercise 10: 8b
4) 200m
5) 84m
6) 17.5km
7) 2m
8) 30m
9) 74m
10) 8km

Exercise 10: 9
1) 66 & 30 marbles
2) 9 : 20
3) 27 children
4) Alex 2, Ben 4, Colin 12
5) 4.5cm
6) 22.5m
7) 4 stickers
8) 45km
9) 2 yrs 3 months
10) a) 205 stickers
    b) 85 stickers

PROGRESS CHARTS

Shade in your score for each exercise on the graph. Add up for your total score. If there are a) b) c) etc. parts to a question, all parts must be correct to gain a mark.

9. PERCENTAGES

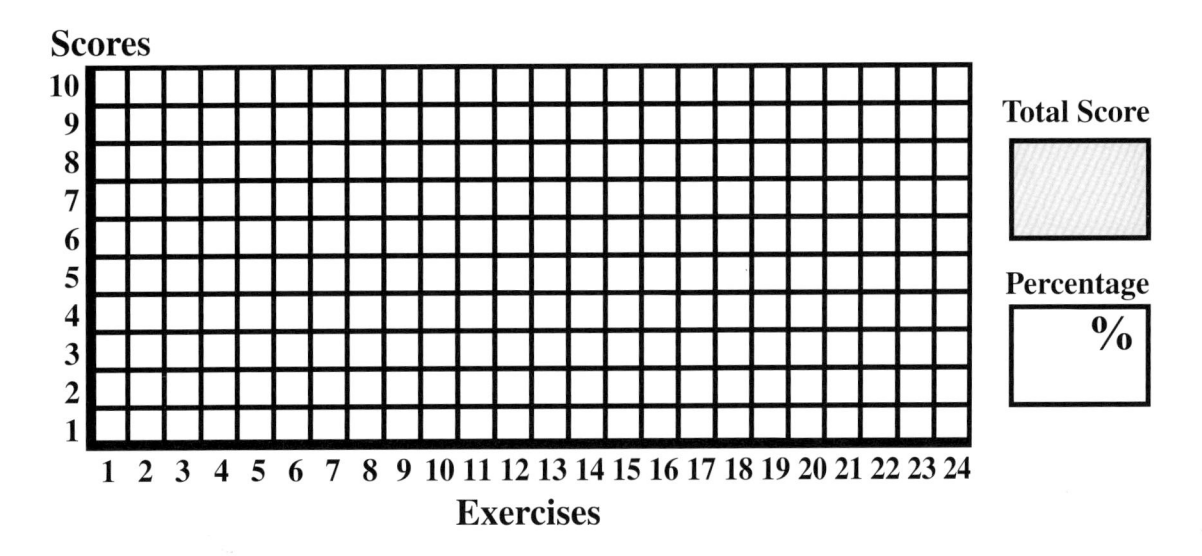

Scores (1–10) vs Exercises (1–24)

Total Score: ☐

Percentage: ☐ %

10. RATIO AND PROPORTION

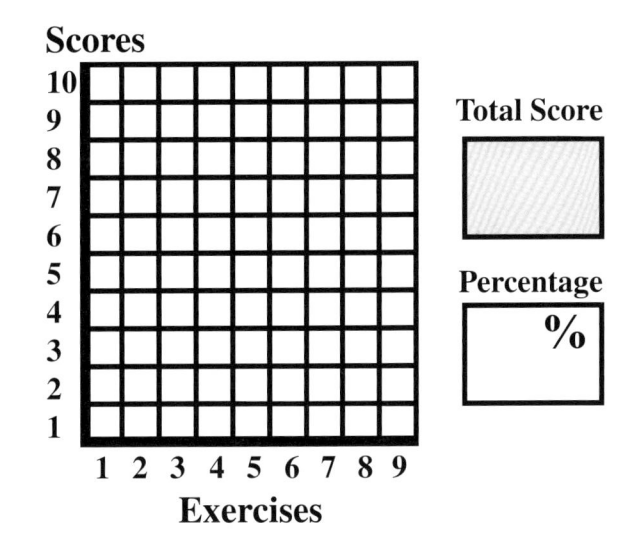

Scores (1–10) vs Exercises (1–9)

Total Score: ☐

Percentage: ☐ %

For the average add up % and divide by 2

Overall Percentage

☐ %

© 2006 Stephen Curran

CERTIFICATE OF
ACHIEVEMENT

This certifies

_____

has successfully completed

11+ Maths
Year 5–7
WORKBOOK 3

Overall percentage score achieved [ ] %

Comment _____

_____

Signed _____
(teacher/parent/guardian)

Date _____

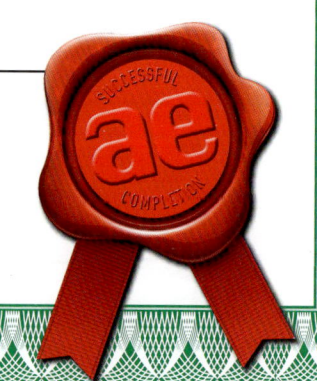